The Making of Kings

Get yourself ready for the coming Kingdom Age.

Winston Lucien Daniels

Order this book online at www.trafford.com
or email orders@trafford.com

Most Trafford titles are also available at major online book retailers.

Printed in Victoria, BC, Canada.

ISBN: 978-1-4269-0541-4 (sc)
ISBN: 978-1-4269-0542-1 (hc)
ISBN: 978-1-4269-0543-8 (eb)

*Our mission is to efficiently provide the world's finest, most comprehensive book publishing
service, enabling every author to experience success. To find out how to publish your book, your
way, and have it available worldwide, visit us online at www.trafford.com*

Trafford rev. 1/21/2010

Trafford
PUBLISHING® www.trafford.com

North America & international
toll-free: 1 888 232 4444 (USA & Canada)
phone: 250 383 6864 ♦ fax: 812 355 4082

Contents

Acknowledgements

I am extremely grateful to Jesus Christ my Lord and Saviour for the transformation work in my own life: "I could never have imagined this".

I thank my wife **Yolande** with whom I have truly become one in not just spirit and body, but more importantly, in our souls. Thank you for enduring the continued process of becoming.

I am ever grateful to my two sons, Jade and Caleb who have offered me so unselfishly to be poured out as a drink offering unto the local household of faith, and now the nations – your inheritance is laid up in store.

To my ever-praying and fasting mom, my dad and brothers, thanks for being my training ground in the initial stages of my personal development and loving me unconditionally.

I thank my Executive Leadership team who continues to push me into the destiny God has for me, having freed me up to go to the different nations to proclaim the message of the Kingdom of God as you took responsibility for the corporate vision.

To all the house of Alpha & Omega Life Centre, thank you for being the platform for me to walk in and excel in that which 'Papa' has purposed for me, and for all the love and support you have shown towards me.

To my Editor in Australia, Mary Gray - I am deeply grateful for the tiresome work, long hours and encouraging feedback provided to me during this journey.

To the men and women and entire five-fold ministry, who have greatly impacted my life, especially on a personal level and through the platform of KMNI (Kingdom Ministries Network International). I appreciate and hold you in high esteem Apostle John M. Boney (Miami, Florida - USA) who has been an Apostolic Father to me and Dr Vincent Valentine (Cape Town, South Africa) and Prophet David Clementson (Texas, USA) for the impact that your life and ministry have made on my life and the ministry of Alpha & Omega International. Thanks for being LID-LIFTERS in my life.

To Joan Peters (VWSA Leadership Development & Educational Institute), for the invaluable opportunities to develop my leadership through meaningful projects and for practically portraying what it is to be a leader, especially in the heat of the moment. Thanks for the immense learning I had under your mentorship.

I will forever be grateful for my divine connection with Apostle Israel Onoriobe who has become a true covenant friend to me. His high work ethic and sacrificial productive lifestyle has challenged me to take a bold step in the direction of becoming a writer, which has brought me my greatest joys, satisfaction and fulfillment.

Foreword

Over the last few years, I have had the privilege of ministering with Winston Lucien Daniels and his spiritual sons in their local assembly, as well as having him on board as a team member on our international ministry to the nations. I know him and it is a blessing to recommend his ministry and the thoughts that are penned down in this book.

Indeed, we are in a new season in God and the clarion call is to minister the true gospel message and establish the Kingdom of God in the earth. Much of what has been declared as the gospel of the Kingdom is a product of man's limited knowledge and understanding. It does not produce the fullness of the purposes of God in the earth because it is inadequate and gives only partial treatment to the trumpetings from the "excellent glory".

This new season demands a new word and a radical change in leadership. There is *"now revelation of the mystery"* that is being manifested in the earth for the obedience of faith (Romans 16:25-26). Therefore the ministry must experience a *shift* that will bring forth a global reformation in the Church. It is a paradigm shift that will allow an apostolic transition into the Kingdom that will change the old wineskin so that the new wine can be preserved for God's purpose and glory.

I trust that you will receive this book with a readiness of mind, and by the searching of scriptures there will be a confirmation to the word that will result in the advancement of God's Kingdom in your life and on a global scale.

Apostle Israel Onoriobe

Introduction

This book specifically deals with the gospel of the kingdom of God and its inherent mysteries. 'Gospel' means 'good news' or 'glad tidings', and it is also the power of God, which is the ability of God to make wonderful things happen for mankind. The kingdom of God in the true sense, is good news to mankind, because it promises to restore the rule of God in our lives, our marriages, our families, our communities, our nations and the entire world we live in. The rule of God is righteous; therefore it produces peace and joy in the lives of those who are willing to make God their ultimate King and Ruler. God's rule in our lives automatically brings us back into rulership, so that we rule over our life's circumstances instead of being ruled by circumstances, problems, persecution, trial, tribulations and adversity.

Jesus was raised from the dead and is now seated at the highest place of honour, power and glory, far above all principalities, powers, might, rule, dominion and every name that is named in the heavens, on the earth and under the earth. Above all, He also raised us up together and made us sit together with Him in heavenly places – we too are seated above all principalities, powers, might, rule, and dominion. The message of the kingdom of God challenges us to live in accordance with the above mentioned reality, which is a kingdom reality.

It is for this very reason the message of the kingdom of God has been Jesus' primary message; because He came to produce kingdom rulers who should take back the earth from the one who took it from Adam and Eve. I have observed over the many years that people become like the preaching and teaching they listen to; therefore it makes perfect sense that Jesus majored on the message of the kingdom of God. Preaching and teaching influences our way of thinking – for as a man thinks, so is he.

There is only **one** gospel message, and this message has different emphases; i.e. the gospel of God, (Romans 1:1) the gospel of Jesus Christ the Son of God, The beginning of the gospel of Jesus Christ, the Son of God; (Mark 1:1) the gospel of the grace of God, But none of these things move me, neither count I my life dear unto myself, so that I might finish my course with joy, and the ministry, which I have received of the Lord Jesus, to testify the gospel of the grace of God. (Acts 20:24) the gospel of Christ, (Romans 1:16) the gospel of peace, And how can men preach unless they are sent? As it is written, "How beautiful are the feet of those who preach good news!" (Romans 10:15) the gospel of the kingdom of God And this gospel of the kingdom will be preached throughout the whole world as a testimony to all nations; and then the end will come. (Matthew 24:14) and the gospel of salvation. For I am not ashamed of the gospel: it is the power of God for salvation to every one who has faith, to the Jew first and also to the Greek. (Ephesians1:13/ Romans 1:16) It is very interesting to note that the message regarding the rapture is not regarded as the gospel message – the rapture is therefore not good news according to the scriptures.

I consider it vitally important for us to understand the plan and purpose of God regarding each of these different kinds of emphases of the gospel (good news) message in order for the Church to be effective and to work together in unity and understanding, not contradicting each other. If we lack this understanding, we might fall into the trap of competing with each other in terms of what is the most important gospel to preach. We are not here on earth to compete with each other but rather, to complete each other.

Jesus is the author and finisher of our faith and He alone is a perfect example to look to and to follow. Jesus clearly defined the reason His Father sent Him and also which gospel message He was here to preach. He also gave His New Testament disciples plus His last days' disciples, direct and clear instruction on what message they ought to preach to all the nations of the world. (Luke 4:43; Luke 9:2; Matthew 10:16) This gives us a clear picture and understanding of what we ought to consider the most important gospel message. If Jesus is the first brother among many, then the many ought to do exactly what the first born has done. Jesus has made the kingdom of God His greatest priority and He commanded us to do the same. But seek ye first the kingdom of God, and his righteousness; and all these things shall be added unto you. (Matthew 6:33) The essence or heart beat of the entire Bible is all about the King of kings, His glorious kingdom and the sons of the kingdom of God.

The gospel of God is indeed good news, because the God who has created the heavens, the earth and the sea and everything in it, promised to be our God. Wow, that is so awesome! The God who created everything, also has the power to recreate our broken messed up lives, and it is this same power that transforms our lives into a master-piece and a testimony of His power and glory. For this is the covenant that I will make with the house of Israel after those days, saith the Lord; I will put my laws into their mind, and write them in their hearts: and I will be to them a God, and they shall be to me a people: (Hebrews 8:10) Through Jesus Christ we can become children of God, But as many as received him, to them gave he power to become the sons of God, even to them that believe on his name: (John 1: 12) – and that is the gospel of God.

The gospel of Jesus Christ the Son of God, is also good news. God the creator of the universe has found it in His heart to love the world so much that He gave His only begotten Son to die in our place. The wages of sin is death, therefore we should all die (be cut off from God), *For the wages of sin is death but the gift of God is eternal life through Jesus Christ our Lord. (Romans 6:23)* but Jesus was willing and obedient to the point of death to die in our place. This gospel is the gospel of salvation, – Jesus died and rose again and is now seated at the right hand of the Majesty on high.

The purpose of the gospel of salvation is to transfer mankind out of the kingdom of darkness into the kingdom of God, nothing more and nothing less. Therefore this message cannot be the only message we should focus on. The gospel of salvation is but just the beginning, yet too much focus have been placed on the gospel of salvation, even after people have been saved for many years. And too much attention has been given to the benefits of salvation instead of the **purpose** of our salvation. The purpose of our salvation is to establish the kingdom of God in every sphere of our lives. The Greek word for salvation is 'soteria', which means prosperity, peace (wholeness and completeness), deliverance, healing, well being, and preservation. All these benefits are the responsibility of the believer to work them out for themselves and not to be taught over and over. Philippians 2: 12 speaks about the fact that we should all work out our own salvation with fear and trembling. However, instead of a discipling focus, the benefits of our salvation have become the most important messages that are being preached by many. The benefits of our salvation must be worked out by the individual in the same way we are saved, which is by believing in our heart and by confessing with our mouth that Jesus Christ is Lord. *For man believes with his heart and so is justified, and he confesses with his lips and so is saved (Romans 10:10)* In the same way we work out the other benefits of our salvation by believing in our heart all those same benefits, and by confessing them with our mouth. Consistent confession will eventually bring possession of the benefits of our salvation as we allow ourselves to suffer long at times.

We should not make the gospel of salvation our camping place, because the kingdom of God is our destiny. This means we will have to stop feeding only on messages that speak about our benefits – the purpose of our benefits is to empower us to fulfill God's purpose, which is to establish the kingdom of God upon the earth. Blessed be the Lord, who daily loads us with benefits, even the God of our salvation. Selah. (Psalm 68:19)

The Gospel of the grace of God is wonderful good news to the hearer of it, especially if we stop to consider what it was like to live under the law of Moses. Can you ever imagine living under the law of 'an eye for an eye and a tooth for a tooth'? For the grace of God that bringeth salvation hath appeared to all men. (Titus 2:11) The grace that has appeared to all men is God's riches at Christ's expense. In order to be free from the law there had to be death. Jesus came to fulfill the law and to release us from it through His death. The message of grace is important to help believers overcome tendencies of dead works, self-righteousness and legalism. We are justified by His grace; therefore anything we would ever need, want and desire will come to us by grace....... through faith: and that not of yourselves: it is the gift of God: Not of works, lest any man should boast. (Ephesians 2:8-9; Titus 3:7)

This understanding removes strife and competition and will cause us to cease from our own works and learn to enter into finished works as we mix the Word with faith. Believers who struggle to understand this will continue to struggle to mature in their Christian walk and their relationship with the Father and others. The kingdom of God is not for achievers, but for believers who have the childlike faith to believe in everything written in the Word of God. The gospel of grace is also not a camping place; therefore we should come to grips with grace by faith and not by our works, but we also need to understand that faith without works is dead faith.

The works of faith is obedience to the **spirit of the Word**, as opposed to obedience to the **letter of the Word,** which will only produce dead works, for the letter kills but the Spirit gives life. Understanding this balance will allow us to move on and not to pitch a camp around the gospel of grace. Believe me, grace without faith-action produces timidity and a passive continuous "waiting-on-God" attitude that never gets things done.

The gospel of Christ educates us to understand the power of God. This is good news, because none of us were ever free and protected from burdens and yokes. Christ is the power of God, which according to 1 Corinthians 1: 24 is also known as the anointing and is God's burden-removing, yoke-destroying power. (Isaiah 10:27) The gospel of Christ is good news as our burdens can be removed and our yokes destroyed because of the anointing. Far and beyond this, the anointing upon our lives also protects us from burdens and yokes once they have been removed and destroyed. Even the gospel of Christ is not a camping place, because the purpose of the anointing is for service, nothing more and nothing less. *Bear ye one another's burdens, and so fulfill the law of Christ. (Galatians 6:2)* The Christ dimension sanctifies us and sets us apart from the world; therefore we can boldly declare that we are in the world, but not of the world.

The gospel of peace is the good news that Jesus Christ is the prince of peace and that there can be no peace in the world apart from Him. The gospel of peace is the good news of Shalom, which carries the meaning of prosperity, wholeness and completeness, nothing missing and nothing broken. This is the joy and excitement of the gospel of peace. The peace of God has a positive effect on our lives, whenever we experience it. The peace of God works within us, making us whole and complete, until there is nothing missing and nothing broken. History records no wars during the time frame Jesus was on earth. There was peace because the Prince of peace was on the earth. I have personally witnessed peace coming into the lives of dysfunctional families after they have received Jesus Christ as their Lord and Saviour. The Prince of peace brings and establishes peace in our personal lives, our marriages, our families, our communities and our nations. Shalom.

Failing to get a real grip on the main message of the kingdom of God, reminds me of missing out on a degree or diploma because we have failed to study the main subject. A degree or diploma has many minor subjects, but only one major subject. We will fail the entire year if we fail our major subject, even if we pass all the minor subjects. This can be said about the many different emphases of the good news of the Bible. We may do well in all these different aspects of the gospel message, but if we will fail to walk in the kingdom of God message, we will utterly fail to fulfill God's ultimate purpose.

The end of this current age will not come, neither will Jesus come, until ...this gospel of the kingdom shall be preached in all the world for a witness unto all nations; and then shall the end come. (Matthew 24:14) Let us gladly do what Jesus commanded us to do when ...he said unto them, Go ye into all the world, and preach the gospel to every creature. (Mark 16:15) Believe me, there are many, many, many creatures who have not yet heard the message of the kingdom of God.

The LORD of hosts hath sworn, saying, Surely as I have thought, so shall it come to pass; and as I have purposed, so shall it stand: (Isaiah 14:24) The LORD'S thoughts and plans towards men was and is that they should subdue the earth and have total dominion over all the works of His hands; so shall it come to pass, and as the LORD has purposed in His heart that we should be rulers, so shall it stand. I trust that you will enjoy this journey that I have traveled during the season of writing this book.

Chapter One

LET US KEEP THE MAIN THING THE MAIN THING.

My goal in writing this book is very simple. I want to paint a BIG picture that will rescue many of us who have become terribly lost in all the detail of the Bible. Our schooling has taught us the valuable lesson of the importance of capturing the essence of each subject we study, rather than studying the entire handbook for our exams. Those of us who could not capture the essence of a subject had a hard time studying with clarity and understanding. This same concept applies to understanding God's plan and purpose when reading all the books in the Old and New Testament. It is important to understand the essential message of the Bible in order for our Christianity to make sense to us and to those who observe our lives.

It took a few years of maturity to make sense of what the Church is all about. Why are we here on planet earth? I consider myself being in a somewhat better place now, because I finally got a glimpse of the BIG picture of why I am here and of what the Church is all about. I also submit myself to the reality that God's revelation of His purposes is progressive and forever unfolding. I have also observed that when we backslide out of the Church we do so because Church is not making sense, and we gradually find ourselves slipping into boredom and frustration. The world seems to make more sense to us, and we feel more free to be ourselves, doing whatever we choose. But I have discovered that this same freedom that we think we have found in the world, can really only be found in the Church, and this happens when we truly grasp the big picture of the Father's plan and purpose for humanity.

Without this BIG picture, we walk around aimlessly with a terrible sense of going-no-where In general we get very lost in the detail of life; therefore we really need to see this big picture. This sense of going-no-where is indeed a horrible sense that many believers struggle with, including myself for many years. Proverbs 13: 12a puts it like this: *hope deferred maketh the heart sick*. I have seen believers being at the same place for so many years, while sinners prosper all around them. The BIG picture I am talking about can also be called the VISION of the Father for His beloved children. If we can't see His VISION we will be lost in a dying world. King Solomon puts it like this: *where there is no vision, the people perish. (Proverbs 29:18)*

A vision can be defined as a mental picture of a preferable future, which is a hundred times better than your current life. This possibility exists if we can take hold of the Father's VISION for us, enabling us to walk in the truth of Ephesians 3:20; *now unto him that is able to do exceeding abundantly above all that we ask or think, according to the power that worketh in us.*

The Father can do for you what you never thought or could have imagined beyond your wildest dreams and expectations, all according to His riches in glory by Christ Jesus. But we desperately need a glimpse of the Father's VISION for our lives. We have many messages which may have had the tendency to contradict each other, adding more confusion. I will clarify the message that Jesus said should be preached, which is the message that is painting the BIG picture of the Father's VISION.

Let's have a look at the concept of a jig-saw puzzle. Unless you can see what the completed picture will look like when finished, it is really difficult to do the puzzle. You will get frustrated and eventually give up. But if you can first scrutinize an image of that BIG picture, you will then have the capacity to put all the small pieces together and to finally complete the BIG picture puzzle.

Big picture thinking is what we call 'contextual thinking' or 'right brain thinking'. Detail thinking is what we call 'content' or 'left brain thinking'. To be able to accomplish something of great worth we need big picture thinking as well as detail thinking. Leadership deals with big picture thinking; management deals with detail thinking. Leadership plus management equal great capacity to do great things. This is what it takes to accomplish something of great worth. We desperately need BIG picture thinking as well as a detailed plan concerning the plan and purpose of God. This is the conclusion of the matter: **Context plus content equals capacity to do great things.**

Far too many of us have become lost in the detail of God's plan; the detail being Church activity and all the different messages we have heard. Most of those messages deal only with the detail of the Father's plan. The message that paints the BIG picture has not yet been preached with the same intensity, clarity and priority. That's why we are lost in all this detail, not seeing the BIG picture. Believe me – the Father is raising up men and women who have seen the BIG picture of His original purpose, and who are preaching the message that Jesus preached during His earthly ministry. The message I am talking about is the message of the kingdom of God that Jesus said His Father had sent Him to preach. *And he said unto them, I must preach the kingdom of God to other cities also: for therefore am I sent. (Luke 4:43)* It is for this purpose the Son of Man came, to show us the BIG picture of the Father's original purpose. Dying on the CROSS was only a means to an end and to give back to us what Adam and Eve lost.

I have now set the platform to paint the BIG picture, which will help cause the detail that has produced so much confusion, to fall into place. This will give us the capacity to live in the kingdom and to establish the kingdom of God upon the earth.

Remember, it takes both big picture and detail thinking to accomplish great things for God. Please kiss confusion goodbye, because we will from now on live with purpose and vision.

The book of Genesis is the book of beginnings, which is a good place to start! It is here that we discover the Father's original purpose and intent. After creating the universe and the planet on which we live, the Creator handed leadership of the earth over to humankind. Genesis 1: 26 explains this very clearly - *And God said, Let us make man in our image, after our likeness: and let them have dominion over the fish of the sea, and over the fowl of the air, and over the cattle, and over all the earth, and over all creepers thing that creeping on the earth.*

What does God really say when He said, 'let them have dominion'? To find the answer we need to understand what 'kingdom' means. *A kingdom is a domain over which a king has rulership.* **Domain** is the root word for **dominion**, which literally means God had given Adam and Eve a kingdom or a domain to rule. The Garden of Eden was their domain or kingdom, but it was only a starting place, a training ground to equip them to branch out into the rest of the world. The Hebrew writer confirms the fact that we have received a kingdom which cannot be moved. *Wherefore we receiving a kingdom which cannot be moved, let us have grace, whereby we may serve God acceptably with reverence and godly fear* (Hebrews 12:28) The writer of the book of Matthew said to us that this glorious kingdom has been prepared for us before the foundation of the earth. *Then shall the King say unto them on his right hand, Come, ye blessed of my Father, inherit the kingdom prepared for you from the foundation of the world.* (Matthew 25:34)

Genesis 1: 28 defines God's assignment for Adam and Eve; God gave them a kingdom and an assignment, therefore we can conclude that they had received a *kingdom assignment or kingdom mandate:- And God blessed them, and God said unto them, Be fruitful, and multiply, and replenish* the earth, and subdue it: and have dominion over the fish of the sea, and over the fowl of the air, and over every living thing that moves upon the earth. Here is an important key point regarding their assignment. They did not work to make a living, because by delighting themselves in the LORD, the blessing took care of whatever they had need of, plus all of their wants and desires. I sought the LORD, and he heard me, and delivered me from all my fears. (Psalm 37:4)

They worked to fulfill their kingdom assignment. The fall of man has perverted the original purpose and intent of work. Today the majority of humanity is working to make a living and work is taking up most of their time, effort and energy, so that they have no time for the assignment on the earth. The purpose of work is to fulfill our earthly assignment and the blessing is supposed to take care of everything we need, want and desire.

LET'S BULLET POINT THE PURPOSE OF WORK FOR THE SAKE OF GREATER CLARITY.

There was no such a thing as sweat in the Garden of Eden. Sweat was and is the result of the curse when they had to toil and labour for their provision outside the Garden of Eden. In the sweat of thy face shalt thou eat bread, until thou return unto the ground; for out of it was thou taken: for dust thou art, and unto dust shalt thou return – (Gen 3:19). This was and is not God's original intent for us to work hard to make a living. Jesus came to restore God's original intent by dying on the cross for us – He sweat blood to redeem us from the curse of sweat - And being in an agony he prayed more earnestly: and his sweat was as it were great drops of blood falling down to the ground - Luke 22:44.

We must work to:

- o fulfil our life purpose;
- o release and maximize our human potential;

o do kingdom business in our workplace;

o receive seeds (salary) to have seed to sow seeds to meet our needs; God gives seed to the sower – See 2Co 9: 10;

o Discover our life calling and life purpose because activity reveals many things about ourselves (being indolent is why lazy people never get to know themselves.)

o acquire skills, life experiences and develop our talents and abilities;

o Submit to unpleasant work which cleanses us, because unpleasant work reveals our shortcomings and negativity. Most of us must first go through unpleasant work while we search to discover the work we are created to do as our kingdom assignment. I am one of them who had to go through the path of unpleasant work for many years, but I have been cleansed and made ready for my kingdom assignment work.

OUR KINGDOM OR PRIMARY ASSIGNMENT:

The Message Bible contains a very interesting translation of our kingdom assignment. **God blessed them: "Prosper! Reproduce! Fill Earth! Take charge! Be responsible for fish in the sea and birds in the air, for every living thing that moves on the face of Earth."** (Prosper – reproduce – fill the earth – take charge – be responsible.)

Prosper – Reproduce – Fill the earth – Take charge – Be responsible over all the works of His hands.

- Be fruitful
- Multiply
- Replenish the earth
- Subdue the earth
- Have dominion over all the works of God's hands, except humankind.

God commanded both male and female to have dominion. This means both men and women have been given the ability and authority to rule and reign together. It also means that we have been created to lead together, not leading each other, but subjecting our leadership to the leadership of God alone.

I have no doubt that Jesus reminds us in Matthew 6: 33 about our first assignment when He says, seek ye first the kingdom of God and His righteousness. In other words Jesus said, we should seek to do the first assignment that God has given humanity. There are two things that Jesus said we should seek after– the kingdom of God and His righteousness.

We cannot effectively carry out our kingdom assignment without the gift of righteousness – see Romans 5: 17 if there was not a fall - humankind would have occupied themselves with a kingdom mandate. It is also important to keep this in mind: Sin marred our ability to rule and to lead effectively; however God did not ordain the fall, but He foreknew the fall, and so in His great wisdom He sacrificed His Son before the foundation of the earth. And all that dwell upon the earth shall worship him, whose names are not written in the book of life of the Lamb slain from the foundation of the world. (Revelations 13:8)

Before the foundation of the earth, God made provision for us to be restored back to our original image and likeness, and to be empowered just like God had blessed (empowered) Adam and Eve when He gave them their kingdom assignment. The blessing that Adam and Eve received was an empowerment to carry out their kingdom assignment. The Bible in Basic English (BBE) and other Bible versions use the word 'happy' instead of blessed. I mention this because there is an important lesson I would like to draw from the word happy. Have you ever noticed whenever you are in a state of happiness that everything you do seems to be effortless and easy? That's the exact result of being blessed – if you are blessed everything you do flows easily. That was and is the original purpose of the blessing – God blessed them so that they could effortlessly subdue the earth and rule over all the works of his hands with great ease, while having the time of their lives. Conversely, have you noticed how hard and difficult it is to get a job done when you are in a state of unhappiness or if you are not blessed by God in what you do? The blessing of God is a wonder.

No wonder the Father's restoration plan includes the very same blessing for us that He has bestowed on Adam and Eve to carry out their kingdom assignment. Ephesians 1:3 speaks about this blessing - *Blessed be the God and Father of our Lord Jesus Christ, who hath blessed us with all spiritual blessings in heavenly places in Christ*: With this blessing in and upon our lives we are fully empowered to carry out our kingdom assignment and to do great exploits in His kingdom. Our effectiveness in life is therefore greatly dependent on the blessing or the grace that we have been blessed with in the heavenly places in Christ Jesus. *For if by one man's offence death reigned by one; much more they which receive abundance of grace (blessings) and of the gift of righteousness shall reign in life by one, Jesus Christ* . (Romans 5:17)

The blessing that was on Adam and Eve came on Abraham when God proposed a kingdom business proposal to Abraham. That same blessing immediately flowed into Abraham's life when he accepted this proposal. This is reason enough to consider it very important to know and understand how to keep the blessing flow strong and fresh in and upon our day-to-day life, to be able to reign in life. I shortly want to give some key points to keep in mind on how to keep the blessing flow strong and fresh in our lives.

God blessed them, according to Genesis 1: 28, so that they could be fruitful, multiply, replenish the earth, subdue the earth and have dominion. This was and is the sole purpose of the blessing, which makes rich and adds no sorrow. I am not a blessing preacher, but I am also not a preacher that preaches against blessings and prosperity. In fact I have diligently learned how to keep the blessing flow active, alive and overflowing in my life, so that I can be a blessing to others. LIFE IS EMPTY AND MEANINGLESS IF WE DO NOT CONTRIBUTE OR ADD VALUE TO OTHER PEOPLE'S LIFE AND WELLBEING.

THE FIVE PRINCIPLES THAT CREATE AN ONGOING BLESSING FLOW:

1. OBEDIENCE – blessings always follow every step of obedience. We must be determined to do whatever the Lord tells us to do and we will see how the blessings of the Lord will overtake our lives. *Behold, I have set before you this day.....A blessing, if you obey the commandments of the Lord your God, which I command you this day:* (Deuteronomy 11:27) We must learn to obey whatever the Lord asks us to do or to give. Be careful of a reasoning mind, because reasoning will lead to disobedience. Just do what the Lord tells you to do without trying to understand, understanding will come after you have obeyed the LORD your God.

2. FAITHFULNESS is being consistent in doing what we are assigned to do in the house of the Lord, irrespective of how we feel. This is what God said about His servant Moses - *My servant Moses is not so, who is faithful in all Mine house.* (Numbers 12:7) Can God say the same thing about you? How faithful are you in the house of God? How faithful are you in exercising your ministry gift? How faithful are you in serving your brothers and sisters? *With the faithful You will show Yourself faithful; with the upright man You will show Yourself upright.* (2 Samuel 22:26) *A faithful man shall overflow with blessings, but he who makes haste to be rich shall not be innocent.* (Proverbs 28:20)

3. A PURE HEART - A person with a pure heart is sincere with right motives – it is a heart that wants to serve and please God. When you are pure, you are free from anything that defiles or contaminates. A pure person is unpolluted and genuine. *Keep* thy heart with all diligence; for out of it are the issues of life. (Proverbs 4:23) The blessing of God dwells within our hearts. All issues we experience in life comes from the heart, including the blessing. Unless we keep our heart pure, we won't be able to experience the blessing flow, because any negative thing we have in our heart blocks the blessing flow. It is not easy to guard our heart, but it is essential. Here are some of the things that can defile or pollute; envy; jealousy; unforgiveness; offences; hatred; anger; revengeful thoughts; negativity, rebellion, anxiety, concerns, worries, etc. We must all grow up to guard our heart above all things. Blessed are the pure in heart! for they shall see God. (Matthew 5:8) The blessings that manifest in our lives is one of the ways in which we can see God.

4. TITHING, this is a 10% of your gross income. Why from the gross income? Well, our earthly Government tax is taken from our gross income – why should our heavenly Government be treated any less? And all the tithe of the land, of the seed of the land, or of the fruit of the tree, is Jehovah's. It is holy to Jehovah. (Leviticus 27:30) Bring all the tithe into the storehouse, so that there may be food in My house. And test Me now with this, says Jehovah of Hosts, to see if I will not open the windows of Heaven for you, and pour out a blessing for you, until there is not enough room. (Malachi 3:10)

5. BE A DOER OF THE WORD – it is not enough to read, meditate or to hear the word of God. We must become doers of the Word, by applying the Word in everything we do. In other words our every action and step must be backed up by the word of God. But whoso looketh into the perfect law of liberty, and continueth therein, he being not a forgetful hearer, but a doer of the work, this man shall be blessed in his deed. (James 1:25)

To re-cap: the purpose of the blessing is not to establish a blessing club, but to carry out our kingdom assignment right here and now upon the earth. We do not have to wait for the age to come. We are blessed to be a blessing – to be blessed is the lowest place in the kingdom; to be a blessing is the highest place. What place in the kingdom do you occupy? Praise be to our Father who has blessed us with all spiritual blessings in heavenly places in Christ Jesus. Christ dwells in our hearts by faith according to Ephesians 3: 17, therefore the blessing that is in the heavenly places in Christ Jesus, also dwells in our hearts by faith. This simply means that the blessing is within us. The blessing of Abraham has come upon the Gentiles – you and me - through Jesus Christ. Never allow negativity or a complaining spirit to rob you of your blessing.

NOAH AND THE KINGDOM MANDATE

And God blessed Noah and his sons, and said unto them, Be fruitful, and multiply, and replenish the earth. (Genesis 9:1) This happened after the flood, which was a type or shadow of a new earth. And in this new beginning God did exactly what He did with Adam and Eve, that is, He blessed them with the same blessing, except He did not say **subdue the earth and have dominion.** So God's blessing to Noah and his descendants reveals to us that:-

- The Father did not give up on us concerning our kingdom assignment.
- The Father is very determined to see our primary assignment being carried out upon all the earth. If not, God's original purpose cannot be fulfilled.
- Even though Adam and Eve fell and failed to carry out their kingdom assignment - it was still very possible for them to be **fruitful**, and **multiply**, and **replenish** the earth without redemption and a restoration process.
- God will never expect us to do anything without giving us the power to perform it. Adam and Eve had handed the power to subdue the earth and to have dominion, over to Satan through their act of disobedience; thereafter God did not expect humanity to subdue the earth and

to have dominion, until He sent His Son to restore this ability in us.

- There was and is a definite need for redemption and restoration in order for the entire kingdom assignment to be carried out by man; therefore we can conclude that man has the ability and potential to partially carry out the kingdom assignment independently from God. This is very evident by what humanity achieves without God. Looking at all the state-of-the-art work, excellence and beauty we create in the world, can you imagine what the Church could do if we step into the fullness of our kingdom assignment. What we see achieved 'in the natural', is just a drop in the ocean in comparison to what is possible for us to accomplish with God's mandate on the earth.

- The lamb that was slain before the foundation of the earth had to come to the earth and die physically, in order to regain the kingdom power that Adam and Eve had handed over to Satan.

- Jesus did come, giving back the power and authority to subdue the earth and to have dominion, but it is also true that we do not access this power all at once, because we are subject to a development restoration process.

- It is this restoration process that has created the need for a secondary assignment, which is an **apostolic assignment** as recorded in Matthew 28: 19-20. **Go ye therefore, and teach all nations, baptizing them in the name of the Father, and of the Son, and of the Holy Ghost: Teaching them to observe all things whatsoever I have commanded you: and, lo, I am with you always,** *even* **unto the end of the world. Amen.**

Chapter Two

THE FIRST SHALL BE LAST AND THE LAST SHALL BE FIRST

Where there is a 'primary' there is generally a 'secondary' and so it is with our assignments from our Heavenly Father. His primary assignment for us cannot be carried out unless we first submit ourselves to our secondary assignment. Our secondary assignment has been designed to make us fruitful. Fruitfulness is the starting point of our kingdom assignment – be fruitful, multiply, replenish the earth, subdue the earth and have dominion. This means each individual believer should be discipled and should disciple others to carry out their secondary assignment, in order for us to be equipped for our primary assignment. Our secondary assignment is a practical strategy to restore mankind back to its original image and likeness in order for us to carry out our primary or, kingdom assignment.

This secondary assignment is the Apostolic Assignment, which precedes our Kingdom Assignment (primary assignment). **The first shall be last; and the last shall be first.** Our kingdom assignment is our first assignment which is now last, and the apostolic assignment which is last is now first; *Till we all come in the unity of the faith, and the knowledge of the Son of God, unto a perfect man, unto the measure of the stature of the fullness of Christ: (Ephesians 4:13)* **Only then,** we will be prepared to fulfill our first assignment completely. I am not saying that we cannot fulfill our kingdom assignment right now, but God's restoration work will surely make us more effective and efficient.

Adam and Eve and every other man after Adam could not completely carry out their first assignment, except the Son of Man; therefore there is a need for every man to grow up unto the measure of the stature of the fullness of Christ, so that He can be the first among many brethren. He was the first MAN who successfully completed His kingdom assignment on the earth; therefore we are the many brothers that will do even greater works than what Jesus did on the earth. Jesus Himself said so. *Verily, verily, I say unto you, He that believed on me, the works that I do shall he do also; and greater works than these shall he do; because I go unto my Father (John 14:12)*

PRIMARY ASSIGNMENT – KINGDOM ASSIGNMENT

And God blessed them, and God said unto them, Be fruitful, and multiply, and replenish the earth, and subdue it: and have dominion over the fish of the sea, and over the fowl of the air, and over every living thing that moveth upon the earth (Genesis 1:28)

- Be fruitful
- Multiply
- Replenish the earth
- Subdue the earth
- And have dominion over everything that God has created, except human beings.

SECONDARY ASSIGNMENT – APOSTOLIC ASSIGNMENT

Go ye therefore, and teach all nations, baptizing them in the name of the Father, and of the Son, and of the Holy Ghost: Teaching them to observe all things whatsoever I have commanded you: and, lo, I am with you always, even unto the end of the world. Amen. (Matthew 28:19-20)

- Go to all the nations in the world
- Make disciples of all the nations
- Teaching them everything Jesus taught us
- Baptizing them in the name of the Father, and the Son, and of the Holy Ghost.

HOW DO WE GO ABOUT MAKING DISICIPLES?

We make disciples by bringing a sense of discipline and focus into people's lives. Most people are undisciplined, especially when they were living unproductive lives before conversion and those who might have been actively involved in activities that requires focus and discipline. Making disciples is easier said than done, because it is not an easy thing to bring discipline into undisciplined people's lives.

This is one of the reasons why only a few ministries are actively involved in making disciples, because most believers in general would rather go to Churches where leaders do not put too much pressure on their flesh. Going to Church on Sundays and doing their own thing from Monday to Saturday is what many believers prefer. Even some of Jesus' disciples left Him, because the force of discipline break or make a person. From that time many of his disciples went back, and walked no more with him – *From that time many of his disciples went back, and walked no more with him. (John 6:66)*. It is very interesting to notice that the scripture reference that refers to those who did not become disciples of Jesus is the number 666.

Seek to find your own revelation concerning this. Those of us who will follow Him to the end will be sealed on our foreheads with the mark of God – see Rev 7: 3. You have no need to fear the mark of the beast (666) if you are sealed with the mark of God.

Making disciples is getting very close to people, which will eventually reveal their undisciplined habits and lifestyle that can become an uncomfortable and uneasy situation. This is far more than looking nice at Church; we get to know the real person through applied discipline. When it comes to people's lives, you can't make a real difference from a distance. Making disciples is about investing time, energy and effort, interaction and building relationships like Joshua and Moses, Elijah and Elisha, Paul and Timothy and Titus. Jesus clearly says we are His disciples **if** we continue in His word; love one another; take up his cross; lose your life for His sake and bear fruit - (John 8: 31; 13: 35; 15: 8). These are all hard core issues that demands absolute discipline from a disciple, which is a person that wants to go beyond being a mere believer. I always get lost in speaking about this important subject, yet my intention is not to go too far regarding this.

Making disciples is to focus on the whole person – body, soul and spirit including other aspects of a person's life, which is mental, vocational, financial, physical, family and social. All these aspects of a person's life must be building upon the word of God, that is to say, getting two or three scripture verses about each of these aspects of life to become rooted and grounded in the Word. In the mouth of two or three witnesses shall every word be established - 2Co 13:1b. The Word of God in our hearts has the power and authority to bring discipline and establishment into all these areas of our lives. Wherewith shall we cleanse our way? By taking heed thereto according to thy words. Thy word I have hid in mine heart, that I might not sin against thee - Psalm 119:11. The word in our hearts and a disciplined life is a buffer against the temptation of sin.

LET US SEEK TO UNDERSTAND THE PURPOSE OF OUR SECONDARY ASSIGNMENT AND THE APOSTOLIC MINSTRY GIFT TO THE BODY OF CHRIST.

Why am I saying that Matthew 28: 19-20 is an apostolic assignment? I am saying so because an apostle is a sent one (they go); therefore everyone who participates in this assignment is apostolic. The apostolic assignment is an international (GLOBAL) calling. This is what we ought to do – we are not called to build Churches, because Jesus clearly said that <u>He will build His Church</u> and the gates of hell will not prevail against Her. We are however called to **plant** Churches. Except the LORD build the house, they labour in vain that build it. (Psalm 127:1a)

Our concern should not be our ministries, but the nations, while Jesus concerns Himself with the building of His Church. If we reverse this order by making our desire to grow a ministry our main focus, the gates of hell will prevail against our ministries. The gates of hell will not prevail against our ministries if we allow Jesus to build His Church. Also take to heart what Paul said; I have planted, Apollos watered; but God gave the increase. (1Corinthians 3:6) This verse clearly defines our responsibility in the process of building the Church – we are assigned to plant and to water. And as we have seen, Jesus will build His Church and God will give the increase.

Many Church growth seminars provide strategies of how to increase membership, yet 1 Corinthians 3: 6 clearly says, that **God** will give the increase. If we follow church growth strategies, we might experience increase, but it will not be lasting because another ministry might also apply the same strategy, and with people tending to go from church to church, there will be no balance. Therefore this kind of increase is obviously unhealthy as our ministries can only grow and develop by being exposed to the variety of ministry God has placed in the Body. Without this exposure we might think we are growing, but actually we are just swelling!

However, when God is giving the increase, those who join us will easily connect with the ASSIGNMENT of the ministry. On the other hand, the people we try to add will eventually leave, because they will struggle to connect with the assignment of the ministry. King David was not overly excited when men came to join him; instead he questioned their inner motives, because he trusted God to bring the increase. Waiting on God requires much patience and long suffering, because he who believes is not hasty. Haste is a sure sign of unbelief and unbelief is sin, and sin in itself creates many, many problems. What really counts are not the numbers we count, but the number of people on whom we can really count on.

Jesus proved this point when He challenged the multitudes that followed Him to increase their level of commitment by taking up their cross. The crowd left and only His twelve disciples stayed behind; they were the ones He could count on. They were also the ones that people said, that they were turning cities upside down. The LORD can do far more with a few committed groups of people than with many thousands of uncommitted half-hearted followers.

The purpose of the Apostolic and the Prophetic is to lay a foundation for the rest of the ministry gifts to build a house for God on the earth for humanity to be restored to their original image and likeness. Jesus said He will build His Church and He does it through the working together of the five-fold ministry gifts. This magnificent house cannot be completed unless the apostles and prophets lay the foundation; *and are built upon the foundation of the apostles and prophets, Jesus Christ himself being the chief corner stone.* (Ephesians 2:20)

Let us also keep in mind that **we** are the house of God. *In whom ye also are builded together for a habitation (dwelling place) of God through the Spirit.* (Ephesians 2:22) **Each of us is a building block in this house – a house that will bring total** restoration to mankind, so that the glory of God covers the earth as the waters covers the sea. *You also, as lively stones, are built up a spiritual house, an holy priesthood, to offer up spiritual sacrifices, acceptable to God by Jesus Christ. (1Peter 2:5)*

Another purpose of the apostolic ministry is to be fathers to the fatherless. One cannot give what he or she does not have, and this is the root cause of not making discipling the main focus in a ministry. Many pastors have never been discipled; consequently they lack the experience and skill to disciple their followers, and this wide-spread weakness cripples the Church's ability to carry out her apostolic assignment. The ministry of the saints, which is to edify or build up the Body of Christ, is therefore neglected. It is not the five-fold ministry's responsibility to build up the Body of Christ; rather they are to equip the saints, so that the saints might build each other up. One man cannot be in close relationship with all the other members of the Body, but as we all relate to those around us, as Christ would have us do, we are then able to build each other up.

It is the Apostolic ministry that has the grace to bring together the five-fold ministry to function together as a team. This is Jesus' intended purpose of the five-fold ministry. The Body of Christ has operated as a three-cylinder engine over the many years, which has affected its ability to come into the abundance of grace that is necessary for ruling and reigning. The Body of Christ is actually a **five**-cylinder engine (apostles, prophets, evangelists, pastors and teachers); an engine with unlimited power to equip the saints to do the work of the ministry, *till we all come into the unity of the faith, and of the knowledge of the Son of God, unto a perfect man, unto the measure of the stature of the fullness of Christ: (Ephesians 4:13)*

The three-cylinder engine was the evangelist, pastor and teacher, trying to do what the five-cylinder engine is designed to do. But God, because of His great love towards us, has restored the prophetic and the apostolic ministry to the Body of Christ, so that we can now operate as a five-cylinder engine. No other ministry gift, other than the apostolic, has the grace to bring the five-fold ministry together to function as a team; therefore we should not be critical towards the apostolic ministry, believing the deceptive lie that the apostolic ministry has ended with the early Church with the death of the twelve apostles of Jesus Christ. And He (JESUS) gave some, apostles; and some, prophets; and some, evangelists; and some, pastors and teachers; For the perfecting of the saints, for the work of the ministry, for the edifying of the body of Christ: Till we all come in the unity of the faith, and of the knowledge of the Son of God, unto a perfect man, unto the measure of the stature of the fullness of Christ. (Ephesians 4:11-13)

Our ministry gifts are rendered ineffective if we try to operate independently from each other. All the five-fold ministry gifts are **inter**dependent. Unless this team functions together as one we will continue to produce children who are being tossed to and fro, and carried about with every wind of doctrine, by the sleight of men, and cunning craftiness, whereby they lie in wait to deceive. (Ephesians 4:14)

Saints of God, we need apostolic grace to be fathered; we need prophetic grace to bring correction; we need the evangelist to make us fruitful; we need the pastor to bring emotional and mental healing and we need the teacher to be taught the Word. All these grace gifts will bring forth the Christ in us for the world to see HIM for who He really is.

Here is an exercise to reflect on: Over the many years each of us must have at least grown in a specific area of our life into the likeness of Jesus. Can you think about a specific area in your life? If you do, just observe yourself among people and see how that specific area touches people's lives for the good. I have a heightened awareness of areas where Christ has been formed in me – I have also noticed how effective and efficient I am in those areas; therefore I have such an intense hunger and thirst to become more like Him in all other areas of my life, for His name sake and for the sake of His kingdom and His people. His people is your spouse and children, your friendship circle, the members in your congregation, all the members in His Body, and all His unsaved ones and all the captives in prison houses. In other words - all of humanity.

Chapter Three

THE GARDEN OF EDEN TEST

It is a pity that Adam and Eve did not know who they were; neither did they know whose they were. Satan knew that they belong to God. He understood that they were created to represent God on the earth. Even beyond that, Satan also understood that if they were not sure who they were, he could in fact undermine their power to subdue the earth and have dominion over it. Identity is not something to be taken lightly, because 'being' comes before 'doing' - we are human beings, not human doings. Therefore Adam and Eve's ability to subdue the earth and to have dominion was hidden in their identity. Notice that Genesis 1:26 first defines their identity and then what they were supposed to do, that is, being before doing. **And God said, Let us make man in our <u>image, after our </u>likeness (being): and let them <u>have dominion</u> (doing) over the fish of the sea, and over the fowl of the air, and over the cattle, and over all the earth, and over every creeping thing that creepeth upon the earth.** BEING – DOING – HAVING is a pattern worth remembering for the sake of effectiveness and efficiency.

NOTHING IS TRULY OURS UNLESS IT HAS BEEN TESTED.

Adam and Eve's test reveals some important things for us to understand how our enemy operates. First, of all God allowed Adam and Eve to be tested by Satan to see whether they would choose to obey Him. Obedience and disobedience is based on options, which allows us to exercise our power to choose. The two trees, the tree of good and evil and the tree of life were two options to choose from, but God gave them foresight of the best godly option for them. God created them to be free moral agents. We read in Deuteronomy 30: 19 that God has given us the power to choose life or death, blessings or cursing. This choice was set before Adam and Eve – keeping in mind that forced love is a violation; therefore God had allowed them to be able to make a choice to love Him.

Secondly, no product can be released into the market-place unless it is first tested to prove whether it is up to standard, and provides the service for which it was made. Adam and Eve were God's created 'product' beings, made for the purpose of replenishing the earth, subduing and having dominion over it. God allowed the test to check whether they were ready to branch out beyond, because Eden was not to end in the garden. Their kingdom assignment was to subdue the earth and to have dominion over all the works of His hands, and Eden was but a mere prototype of what needed to be done in the rest of world, until the world in its entirety was under the rulership of Adam and Eve. This would have been in alignment with the heavenly rulership of God. Thy kingdom come, Thy will be done in earth, as it is in heaven. (Matthew 6:10)

The garden of the Eden was the first franchise concept in the world. Kentucky, Mac Donalds, etc. understand the franchise concept very well. Unfortunately the story of Adam and Eve had a sad ending, because they actually failed to do exactly what God intended them to do - instead they subjected their whole domain to Satan, making him the god of this world. *In whom the god of this world hath blinded the minds of them which believe not, lest the light of the glorious gospel of Christ, who is the image of God, should shine unto them.* (2 Corinthians 4:4)

The heart-piercing words the prophet Samuel spoken to King Saul is applicable to the situation Adam and Eve found themselves in; *And Samuel said to Saul, Thou hast done foolishly: thou hast not kept the commandment of the LORD thy God, which he commanded thee: for now would the LORD have established thy kingdom upon Israel for ever.* (1 Samuel 13:13) And in the same way Adam and Eve also did foolishly – they did not keep the commandment of the LORD their God, which he commanded them. *And the LORD God commanded the man, saying, Of every tree of the garden thou mayest freely eat: But of the tree of the knowledge of good and evil, thou shalt not eat of it: for in the day that thou eatest thereof thou shalt surely die.* (Genesis 2:16-17) The LORD would have established their kingdom upon the earth forever and there would have not been a sin-problem at all; rather, righteousness and peace and joy in the Holy Ghost would have been the very nature of our natural world, just like heaven. Heaven on earth was and is the Father's plan for man. *That your days may be multiplied, and the days of your children, in the land which the LORD sware unto your fathers to give them, as the days of heaven upon the earth.* (Deuteronomy 11:21)

This brings us to the third reason for Adam and Eve's test in the garden. Keeping in mind that the devil's fall in the first place was because he wanted to exalt his throne above the stars of God. *For thou hast said in thine heart, I will ascend into heaven, I will exalt my throne above the stars of God: I will sit also upon the mount of the congregation, in the sides of the north.* (Isaiah 14:13) Put this together with the understanding, that the devil knew Adam and Eve were God's and that they were created in His image and likeness. He also knew that they were placed in the garden east in eden, to subdue the earth and have total dominion over all the works of God's hands, including Satan himself.

Satan was also very much aware that his attempt to overthrow God had failed, and that both Adam and Eve had an exalted throne above the throne he had occupied in that given moment, which was far below the stars of God. The devil also knew that he was very limited in the environment he found himself, because he was not designed to operate in the earthly realm. This sucker was in a far more vulnerable position than Adam and Eve. How great it would have been if they had realised that the devil was a desperate loser, and that he was waiting for them to fail the test so that he could operate through their dominion-power in order for him to survive in an environment he wasn't designed for. Therefore we can conclude that Adam and Eve's temptation was the devil's strategy to overthrow them, because he was after the kingdom that they had received.

In the same way, the devil tempted Jesus concerning the kingdoms, because he knew Jesus had come to take back the kingdom he had stolen from Adam and Eve. *Again, the devil taketh him up into an exceeding high mountain, and sheweth him all the kingdoms of the world, and the glory of them; And said unto him, All these things will I give thee, if thou wilt fall down and worship me.* (Matthew 4:8-9) How could the devil promise to give Jesus the kingdoms if he did not have control over them? Where did he get all the kingdoms of the world, and the glory of them? Keeping in mind that the devil has no glory of his own – all the kingdoms of the world and their glory, is the kingdom Adam and Eve lost through their disobedience. Another question might be this: If Adam and Eve lost the kingdom, why does the above verse speak about kingdoms, i.e. more than one kingdom? God restored the kingdom to Israel, but it was divided because of their disobedience. And so this One kingdom became many kingdoms.

God clearly instructed Adam and Eve not to eat of the fruit of the tree which was in the midst of the garden, neither to touch it, lest they should die. These instructions were very clear and simple to follow. The devil had no power and authority, not even so much as to speak to Adam and Eve, but God gave him permission in order to test them. Adam and Eve had nothing in common with the serpent - they were superior to the snake and they also had power and authority to exercise dominion over every creeping thing. The devil himself, in the form a snake, was a creeping thing. There is no power which is not of God, and all powers are ordered by God. (Romans 13:1) God gave the devil power to test them. Now let's look at the test: And the serpent said unto the woman, Ye shall not surely die: For God doth know that in the day you eat thereof, then your eyes shall be opened, and ye shall be as gods, knowing good and evil. (Genesis 3:4-5)

This whole conversation reminds me of what Paul said to the Galatians - O foolish Galatians, who bewitched you not to obey the truth. O foolish Adam and Eve, why have you allowed the snake to bewitch you not to obey God's instructions. They were already gods and did not have to do anything to become gods – they were created in the image and likeness of God. They also did not have to know the difference between good and evil – it was good enough for them to know good only. Abstain from all appearance of evil. (Thessalonians 5:22) God did not design man to know evil, and now evil is destroying mankind because we do not have a built-in system to live in an evil environment.

Adam and Eve's kingdom assignment was to establish on earth, the kingdom of God, which is righteousness and peace and joy in the Holy Ghost. (Romans 14:17) There wasn't supposed to be any evil or wickedness upon the earth – only righteousness and peace and joy in the Holy Ghost. It is for this reason God said He will cut off the wicked and the evil doers from the face of the earth. Wait on Jehovah, and keep His way, and He shall lift you up to inherit the earth; when the wicked are cut off, you shall see it. (Psalm 37:34)

Know this thing for sure - the God of peace shall bruise Satan under our feet shortly. This verse in Deuteronomy 17: 7; 12, captures the heart of God concerning evil; **The hands of the witnesses shall be first upon him to put him to death, and afterward the hands of all the people. So thou shalt put the evil away from among you............And the man that will do presumptuously, and will not hearken unto the priest that standeth to minister there before the LORD thy God, or unto the judge, even that man shall die: and thou shalt put away the evil from Israel.**

Adam and Eve's fall is the devil's success story; therefore the devil will continue to use the very same strategy to tempt humanity. This is the key of his success: He will try his very best to occupy our thinking with what we don't have and what we desire to have. If he can get this right, he will also endeavour to take our minds off what we do have, until what we do not have overshadows everything we have. Getting us into this place makes us very gullible to his suggestions.

Adam and Eve were surrounded with great abundance, but the one thing they could not have made them blind to what they had in great abundance. We must become very sensitive and alert to this attack of the devil, and whenever we sense an attack of this sort, we must immediately become conscious of the goodness of the LORD and everything He has done for us. It is even best to write down all the things the LORD has done for you and begin to give Him thanks for everything you have. Just watch and see how the devil will flee from you, because his strategy cannot work when we are conscious of the goodness of the LORD.

Ever since Adam and Eve became disconnected with their true identity, humanity suffered an identity crisis, which produces so much confusion. Now, instead of a sense of righteousness and peace and joy in the Holy Ghost, we are confused as to who we are and whose we are. The time has come for the sons of God to take their rightful place and begin to subdue the earth, exercising their dominion right over all the works of their Father's hands. *For the earnest expectation of the creation waits for the manifestation of the sons of God.* (Romans 8:19)

There is therefore a need for the sons of God to accept their true identity and allow the Father to restore our identity as gods, because in this truth lies hidden the power and authority to subdue the earth and to have dominion. It was Adam and Eve who made him (the devil) the god of this world – it will be us who will dethrone him. All of creation waits for this to happen in the hope of being delivered from the bondage of corruption into the glorious liberty of the children of God. This is the reason the heavens retain Jesus. *And He shall send Jesus Christ, who before was proclaimed to you, whom Heaven truly needs to receive until the times of restoration of all things, which God has spoken by the mouth of His holy prophets since the world began* . **And in the BBE version;** *And that he may send the Christ who was marked out for you from the first, even Jesus: who is to be kept in heaven till the time when all things are put right, of which God has given word by the mouth of his holy prophets, who have been from the earliest times.* (Act 3:20-21)

So we see that God wants everything He has made to be fully and completely restored and He is in no hurry for His Son's second return. Let's reinforce this reality:

- Jesus will return a second time, but not very soon as many have said. Soon is a short time in human terms, but not when God said soon.
- The Father is keeping Jesus in heaven until the times of restoration of **all** things.
- The prophets clearly spoke about the many things that must still be restored. This includes the restoration of the kingdom and the sons of the kingdom, in terms of their

ability to subdue the earth and to have dominion over all the works of their Father's hands, delivering the earth from the bondage of corruption into the glorious liberty of the children of God. Until this happens, Jesus will be kept in heaven. Therefore all the RAPTURE teachers may just as well change their message and begin to align themselves with the message of the kingdom of God. *The earth is the LORD'S, and the fullness thereof; the world, and they that dwell therein.* (Psalm 24:1) Why should we escape from the earth and give the earth to the devil, which is exactly what Adam and Eve did. Are we not redeemed to do what Adam and Eve failed to do? The devil has no right to take over the earth, because the earth is the LORD'S and the fullness thereof. TO HELL WITH THE DEVIL!!!

The Church has yet to fully obey the Word of God, which says that every enemy must be put under the feet of Jesus. Not a little bit of victory, but complete victory. If we do not have a victorious mindset, we are in unbelief and we are in sin. The rapture is a sure way to abort total victory over the enemy and his foes.

JESUS SAID WE ARE gods.

It is not enough for us to read only what Jesus said in John 10:34 - *Jesus answered them, Is it not written in your law, I said, Ye are gods?* We should all get a personal revelation of this truth in order for it to set us free from any false identity and every high thought that exalts itself against the knowledge of God. The knowledge of God is what God said about us – we all need a personal revelation that we are indeed gods, according to Psalm 82:6 - *I have said, You are gods; and all of you sons of the Most High.* This is the scripture verse that Jesus quoted from in John 10: 34.

How does this truth about you being a <u>god</u> sound in your ear? Does it sound like blasphemy or heresy in your ears? If it does, you need to shake off that traditional religious spirit that tries to exalt itself against the knowledge of God. It is written that you are a god and a son of the Most High (understanding that a son in the kingdom represent both male and female). Go beyond reading it – meditate upon it, because it is meditation that will bring the revelation. Then take another bold step by confessing the word that says you are a god. Do this until you believe in your heart that according to God, this is what you are. For with the heart one believes and with the mouth confessions are made. The word of God must be in two places – in our heart and in our mouth. This is what we call the word of faith – the word that is in your heart and in your mouth. Why is this so important? It is important because it is not possible to subdue the earth and to have dominion if we see ourselves anything less than gods.

The Israelites could not possess their promised land because they saw themselves as grasshoppers. They had to overcome their identity crisis to be able to subdue the giants in their promised land. I feel for those who are introverts, because I know introverts would naturally struggle to embrace and accept this truth of being a god. I therefore encourage those who are introverts to push beyond those condemning voices and listen to the still small voice that bears witness in your spirit that you are indeed a god to the glory of God the Father.

KING DAVID HAD A PERSONAL REVELATION THAT WE ARE gods.

Let's study king David's revelation to lay a foundation to receive our own personal revelation regarding our god identity. In Psalm 8: 4-6 David asked a couple of questions and it seems he immediately received insight and understanding on these questions. (This also reveals the power of dialogue!) What is man, that thou art mindful of him? and the son man, that thou visitest him? For thou hast made him a little lower than the angels, and hast crowned him with glory and honor. Thou madest him to have dominion over the works of thy hands; thou hast put all things under his feet. (Psalm 8:4-6)

It is very obvious that David had a visitation from God and it makes him wonder why God would visit him. This makes him realize that there must be similarities between him and God. For what other reason would God visit him. A dog has no interest in visiting a cat; neither does a donkey visit a dog. So why would God be mindful of him – a dog is not mindful of a cat, but a dog is very mindful of another dog. Genesis 1: 26 gives an indication of why God visits man – it's because God made man in His image, after His likeness. Dogs give birth to dogs; cats give birth to cats; therefore it is more than right to believe that God gives birth to gods. Why would we want to believe that we are anything less than gods – is it not written in our law that we are gods? God Himself is crowned with glory and honour; therefore He has also crowned us with glory and honour.

1Samuel 28: 12- 14 is a very interesting account that reveals to us that we are truly gods. Saul in his backslidden state went to seek for a woman with a familiar spirit to fulfill the role of a prophet in his life and to call forth Samuel from the grave. It is very interesting to notice what this woman saw when she began to tap into the spirit world. She saw gods ascending out of the earth. And the king (Saul) said unto her, Be not afraid: for what sawest thou? And the woman said unto Saul, I saw gods ascending out of the earth. And he said unto her, What form is he of? And she said, An old man cometh up; and he is covered with a mantle. And Saul perceived that it was Samuel, and he stooped with his face to the ground, and bowed himself. (1 Samuel 28:13-14)

Yes, we are god's - God has made us to have dominion over the works of His hands; He has put all things under our feet.

The Hebrews writer says, *but now we see not yet all things under our feet.* (Hebrews 2:8c) The Father after all did say to His Son, *Sit at my right hand until I make Thine enemies Thy footstool.* (Hebrews 1:13) **If Jesus had to sit and wait for His enemies to be made His footstool and God Himself has appointed mankind to take responsibility of the earth, who then will make Jesus' enemies His footstool? Is it not obvious that we are the people who are responsible to do this?**

God will make Jesus' enemies His footstool by and through us, the Church. Who are Jesus' enemies? Are they not the devil and his foes – the principalities and powers, the rulers of the darkness of this world and spiritual wickedness in high places, the anti-Christ, false prophets and the beast? Jesus has already triumphed over them on the cross *And having spoiled principalities and powers, he made a shew of them openly, triumphing over them in it.* (Colossians 2:15) – **our part is to put them under our feet by subduing the earth and by having dominion over all the works of our Father's hands. We do not yet see all things under our feet, but there will come a time when this will be a reality. We are the Body of Christ; therefore we are the feet of Jesus. God put our feet on Satan's neck, and He wants to see the reality of it in our daily lives.**

If Jesus waited for his enemies to be made His footstool, why would He come back to rescue us from the devil and his foes by means of a RAPTURE? Yes He is coming, but He is not coming to RAPTURE us. He is coming to receive the kingdom which the sons of the kingdom have established, so that He may deliver up the *kingdom to God, even the Father; when He shall have put down all rule and all authority and power.* (1 Corinthians 15:24)

The kingdom message and the so called rapture theory is like water and oil – they are opposing concepts. The kingdom message exhorts us to take over the earth, and the rapture theory attempts to comfort believers about the great escape from the earth to avoid the evil in the world. It contradicts the fact that

Jesus said that we are the salt of the earth and the light of the world. God did not create the earth in vain; He formed it to be inhabited. (Isaiah 45:18)

God also promised to preserve us, so that we can establish the earth, which He has given to the children of men. (Isaiah 49:8) The heaven, even the heavens, are the LORD'S: but the earth hath he given to the children of men. (Psalm 115:16) I consider the rapture as mere wishful thinking. We have no right to claim anything that God did not promise in His Word. There is no scripture verse in the Bible that promises us heaven, but the Word on the contrary does promise heaven on earth. Let us continue to pray for the kingdom of heaven to come upon the earth as it is heaven.

We are indeed living in the times of restoration of all things. Jesus will not come back until all things that the prophets have spoken have been fully and totally restored. In other words, all things must become what the Father has intended them to be from the beginning. The Father's purpose was for Adam and Eve and their offspring to subdue the earth and to have total dominion over all the works of His hands. We also need to keep in mind that the devil is also the works of His hands. Behold, I have created the smith that bloweth the coals in the fire, and that bringeth forth an instrument for his work; and I have created the waster to destroy. (Isaiah 54:16) King David in Psalm 8 adds greater insight to our understanding of the Father's purpose by saying, **He has put all things under our feet** (the feet of the Church). But in reality we do not yet see all things under our feet. This has been the result of the fall of Adam and Eve. Heaven is perfect; there is no work to be done in heaven. The Father wants His people to be on the earth, so that we can reclaim and take back the earth which He has created for our enjoyment. As it is now, nobody is enjoying the earth in the way the Father planned we should!

Our assignment is to create a heavenly culture and a heavenly atmosphere, on earth. Only those who die before the second coming of Christ will have the benefit of going to heaven. Heaven is for dead people who wait for the second coming of Christ to bring them back to earth. The kingdom of God on the earth is for people who are alive and well.

It is important to know and understand that God will never ever contradict Himself in His Word – God is not confused. Let's connect with this common sense: We fully understand according to the parable of the talents recorded in Matt 25: 14-29 that our Father in heaven does not tolerate laziness, so why would He rapture us to go up to heaven to do nothing except worship. Heaven is a perfect place; there is absolutely nothing to be done up in heaven, for there is much work to be done on earth. Going to heaven to do worship only is fine for people who are satisfied with only going to Church without having any intention to be the light in this world. Paul also did not tolerate laziness, which is why he said the following words to the Thessalonians Church: *For even when we were with you, this, we commanded you, that if any would not work, neither should he eat –* (2Th 3:10.) Have you ever heard this song? Some people want to go to heaven, but they are afraid to die. Heaven is for those who die before the 2nd coming of Christ. See you in heaven if we die before Christ's second coming. However, I sincerely hope to see the kingdom of God established on earth, because there are far too many people suffering in this world that needs to see the reality of the kingdom of God for me to think about flying away to heaven.

Those of us who remain will have the glorious privilege to see all things being put under our feet, so that we can give back the kingdom to the Son when He comes back to be the King over all His people; His people who He has made kings and priests. *And hath made us kings and priests unto God and his Father; to him be glory and dominion for ever and ever. Amen. (Revelation 1:6)*

THE CREATOR OF THIS WORLD NEEDS A MAN AND A WOMAN TO DO WHAT HE WANTS TO DO IN THE EARTH.

We have come to understand that the Father has handed rulership over to mankind; therefore God needs a man to do whatever He intends to do on the earth. *The heaven even the heavens are the LORD'S; But the earth hath he given to the children of men. (Psalm 115:16)* The Father slew Jesus before the foundation of the earth to redeem mankind, so that He could restore man back to his original image and likeness, with the ability to subdue the earth and to have dominion over all the works of His hands. But Jesus had to become a man to die for the sin of mankind. But even before the execution of this plan, God chose a man called Abraham and tested his obedience and faith. If Abraham had failed this test, Jesus could not have come to earth until God had found someone to pass His test.

Genesis 22: 1-2 records Abraham's test of commitment. *And it came to pass after these things that God did prove Abraham, and said unto him, Abraham. And he said, Here I am. And he said, Take now thy son, thine only son, whom thou lovest, even Isaac, and get thee into the land of Moriah. And offer him there for a burnt-offering upon one of the mountains which I will tell thee of.* Abraham's willingness to sacrifice his only begotten son set the stage for God to give His only begotten Son as a ransom for many. Isaac was born in an impossible situation – miraculously. Jesus' birth was also supernaturally and miraculously by God's word; He fertilized an egg in the womb of Mary by the power of the Holy Spirit coming upon her, and the seed of Abraham, Jesus Christ, was conceived and born. God was carrying out the Abrahamic covenant by bringing Jesus into the earth through one of Abraham's descendants.

Now – here's the thing; if God needed a man to redeem mankind, why would He now do things any other way? Whatever happens on earth is our responsibility – God will not step in to do what we are assigned to do. The earth is in a terrible mess, but God will not step in because He has given the earth to the children of men. Therefore we can conclude by saying that the condition of the world is a mirror reflection of the condition of the Church. This actually means we have not yet subdued the earth and we do not yet have total dominion over the works of our Father's hands. The rapture is not the remedy for the mess that is in the world – the rulership of God is the remedy – keeping in mind that this rule is the kingdom of God.

THE KINGDOM IS GOD'S PURPOSE AND THE CHURCH IS GOD'S PLAN.

The Church is God's plan, and the kingdom is God's purpose. Most of us have occupied ourselves with much of the detailed plan of God and have missed out on His purposes. When He said 'occupy till I come', Jesus was saying we must do kingdom business until He comes. *And He called his ten servant and delivered them ten pounds and said unto them Occupy till I come (Luke 19:13)* It is very easy to get lost in the detail of His plan without the knowledge of His purpose, especially when we hear so many different kinds of messages dealing with God's plan.

The time has indeed come for us to develop a sharp focus on the message of the kingdom, which deals with the Father's purpose. There is no other message that can effectively prepare the saints to posses the kingdom, neither is there any other message that will direct the Church into Her glorious future. It is so important for us to connect with the theme of the Bible, which is the KING, His kingdom and the sons of the kingdom.

We read in Genesis about the fall of Adam and Eve and in the very same book God begins to seek a man to cut a covenant to send His Son to redeem mankind. All the other books in the Bible are not isolated messages and stories – each book builds progressively upon the purpose of God as recorded in the book of beginnings. All the prophets foretold of the coming of God's Son to the earth to redeem mankind, until it reaches its ultimate climax in the book of Daniel. *But the saints of the most High shall take the kingdom, and possess the kingdom for ever, even for ever and ever. (Daniels 7:18)*

This is truly what it is all about. The saints of the Most High will once again posses the kingdom that Adam and Eve lost in the beginning. Believe me, we have majored on a lot of minor things with no visible kingdom results. Many of us have not yet aligned ourselves with the song that the Father has released in the Church – it is not about us, it is all about Him. Much of what has been preached focuses on us, which was needed for our restoration. *Jesus answered them, "Go and tell that fox: 'I am driving out demons and performing cures today and tomorrow, and on the third day I shall finish my work.' (Luke 13:32)* 'Today' speaks of the season of the deliverance ministry in the Church and 'tomorrow' speaks of the season of the healing ministry to deliver and heal the people of God, but the 'third day' ministry is a total shift in focus. The focus is not on us – the focus is on the Father's business and the work that needs to be finished or perfected. The time has come for us to focus on the Father's purpose and to make it our priority *But seek ye first the kingdom of God, and His righteousness; (Matthew 6:33)*

The Father wants to see His kingdom established upon the earth; He wants to see His children being fruitful, multiplying, replenishing the earth, subduing the earth and having dominion over all the works of His hands and putting all things under our feet. *And the LORD said unto Moses, See, I have made thee a god to Pharaoh. (Exodus 7:1)* Let us keep in mind that Pharaoh represents Satan, therefore the God of the universe will make us a god to Satan, just like Adam and Eve have made Satan the god of this world. Jesus came to reverse the effects of Adam and Eve's mistake so that we can do what Adam and Eve failed to do.

Chapter Four

THE TRUE MINISTRY OF JESUS

The heart beat of Jesus' ministry on planet earth is revealed in three verses of the New Testament. Firstly in Luke 4: 43, which speaks about the reason God the Father sent His only begotten Son; next in Luke 19: 10 where the reason for Jesus' coming and what He seeks for is stated; and lastly in Matthew 4: 17 where, in His first public statement, the preaching of the kingdom is revealed to be His primary message. This last verse is also the central theme of the entire Bible. Everything ever concluded about the Bible needs to be aligned with this central theme of the KINGDOM of God.

A DISCOVERY OF WHAT JESUS CAME TO SEEK AND SAVE.

For the Son of man is come to seek and to save that which was lost. (Luke 19:10) But what was lost, we might ask ourselves. What was it Jesus came to seek and save? Again we have to go back to the beginning of all things to discover the answer, keeping in mind nothing would have been lost if there wasn't a fall. Rather, Adam and Eve would have been too fruitful and productive for anything under their care and oversight to get lost. Their assignment was to work the garden and to take care of it and to guard it. *And the Lord God took the men, and put him into the Garden of Eden to dress it and to keep it.* (Genesis 2:15) Nothing should have been lost, but things did get lost because they had failed to guard the garden properly; therefore the snake called Satan, was able to slip in to tempt them and cause their fall. They did not obey the commandments of the Lord, and so handed over to Satan their ability and authority to subdue the earth and to have dominion. Accordingly, the first thing they lost was the kingdom which God had given them.

The second thing lost was the relationship and intimacy they had with the LORD their God. Read the following account and feel for yourself the brokenness, aloofness and the empty void in Genesis 3: 8-10. *And they heard the voice of the LORD God walking in the garden in the cool of the day: and Adam and his wife hid themselves from the presence of the LORD God amongst the trees of the garden. And the LORD God called unto Adam, and said unto him, Where art thou? And he said, I heard thy voice in the garden, and I was afraid, because I was naked; and I hid myself.* If you are married, can you imagine your spouse hiding himself or herself from you. How would you feel if your partner says to you, I am afraid because I am naked. Hear me saints of God, something precious was taken away from the LORD their God who loved them and created them in His image and likeness. They were no longer practicing the presence of the LORD; on the contrary, they hid themselves from Him.

They stopped creating an atmosphere of praise for God to inhabit. *But thou art holy, O thou that inhabitest the praises of Israel.* (Psalm 22:3) They were now separated from the LORD their God. These two beautiful people, who were the crown of God's creation, now became the servants of sin. (John 8:34) This situation reminds me of what God said to Cain. *If thou do well, shalt thou not receive? but if ill, shall not sin forth with be present at the door? but the lust there of shall be under thee, and thou shalt have dominion over it* (sin).

(Genesis 4:7) They were now servants of sin, instead of having dominion over sin. They had dominion over the snake, but they did not exercise their dominion correctly. They were suppose to tell the snake, "shut your mouth snake and get out of the garden immediately; you have no right to be in this garden". Instead they entered into a conversation with the evil snake, who deceived them into believing his lies. This is a heartbreaking story; no wonder the Father loves the world so much that He gave His only begotten Son to come and die for a dying world and to seek and save that which was lost.

There is no other place to seek to understand what was lost and what Jesus came to seek and save. It is very obvious that Jesus came to seek two lost things, i.e. the **lost kingdom** and the **sons of the kingdom** – you and me. No wonder His first public statement reflected His heartbeat - REPENT FOR THE KINGDOM OF HEAVEN IS AT HAND. (Matthew 4:17) Then He also declared the purpose of His coming I AM SENT TO PREACH THE MESSAGE OF THE KINGDOM OF HEAVEN. (Luke 4:43b)

We generally become like the preaching we listen to; therefore Jesus continuously preached the message of the kingdom of heaven. He came to produce a kingdom people, so that we would be enabled to repossess the kingdom which Daniel saw in a vision. Whosoever listens to healing preaching gets healed; those who listen to deliverance preaching get delivered; those who listen to faith preaching develop strong faith; those who listen to love teaching become very loving people; those who listen to success teaching become successful; etc. But none of the above preaching can produce a peculiar kingdom royal priesthood of people that truly show forth the praises of Him who called us out of darkness into His marvelous light (His Kingdom). It is only the message of the kingdom of God that can produce a kingdom people.

Sense the serious tone when Jesus said, I must preach the message of the kingdom of heaven to other cities also. (Luke

4:43a) All the cities in the world must hear this message of the kingdom of heaven. This means we also must preach this message; but how shall the people in all the other cities hear the message of the kingdom without a preacher. And how shall they preach, except they be sent? And how shall they hear this message if everybody else is preaching messages that do not have the power to produce a kingdom people? Saints of God, it is only the message of the kingdom of God that has the power to produce a kingdom people upon the earth. A kind of people that will arise in the power of His might to establish His kingdom.

It is this message that has the power to restore the ability of MANKIND to subdue the earth and to have total dominion. For indeed the kingdom of God is not in word, but in power. (1 Corinthians 4:20) Power is the ability to make things happen – this message of the kingdom of God has the power to restore our ability to make great and mighty things happen upon the face of the earth. The kingdom of God cannot be established unless we preach its message, thereby releasing Kingdom power and glory.

The many different messages we have heard over the many years have produced a mixture of people in the Body of Christ, but still no actual kingdom people. There have been a few groups who have preached the message of the kingdom of God without compromise. Groups serious about producing a kingdom people who have no ambition to build a big ministry. Their labour and focus has always been geared towards establishing the kingdom of God and producing a kingdom people to the glory of the King of kings.

Those who had a different focus and the ambition to build a big ministry have produced people who are strong in faith, because they have preached the faith message; others have produced a people who have become very successful because they have mostly focused on success principles; some ministries have produced great leaders, because their focus was and is leadership principles; some ministries have produced people that are mighty deliverers, because the word on deliverance was their focus; some have produced great healers and healings, because they gave much attention to the word on healing; some have produced wealthy people, because the word on prosperity, riches and wealth has been their primary focus; some ministers have become mighty men of God, because the supernatural and the miraculous was their primary focus; etc; etc; etc.

This brings me to a very challenging question: Did all these different focuses establish the kingdom of God? Did they make this world a better place that we may all lead a quiet and peaceable life in all godliness and honesty in the fear of God? Unfortunately it is an emphatic NO! It has, without a doubt, made the life of Church people better, but it did not make the world a better place. Jesus on the other hand had a **world** focus, not a Church focus, because the earth and the fullness thereof is the LORD'S. Jesus came to make the entire world a better place; therefore He disarmed principalities and powers. When Jesus said to pray that the will of God be done on earth and for His kingdom to come, He was actually meaning for us to pray for a global takeover, so that all the kingdoms of this world may become the kingdoms of our Lord, and of His Christ (His Body – the Church). God is aware of many other groups that are more determined than the church to take over the world. – groups like the Muslims and the New Age Movements, who desire a One World Global System. But this is the good news - any imitation only reveals the existence of the REAL thing. The kingdom of God is that REAL thing – a one governmental world system that is based on righteousness; a righteousness which produces peace and joy in the Holy Ghost.

THE KINGDOM MESSAGE WILL BRING THE END.

Jesus said the end will come when we preach the message of the kingdom of God in **all** the world for a witness to **all** the nations. (Matthew 24:14) What will this end be or, the end of what? Will it be the end of this world? This is a very important question; therefore we should search the scriptures diligently for the answer, instead of allowing religion or our traditional thinking to inform us. After all, whichever conclusion we come to, the quality and destiny of our lives will be affected accordingly. We find the correct and only answer to this question in Ephesians 3:21 *Unto him be glory in the church by Christ Jesus throughout all ages, world without end. Amen.*

Why am I saying that the answer to this question will affect the quality of our lives? Well, if a person believes that there will come an end to this world, such a person will live differently from a person who thinks this world will never end. The person who thinks this world will never end will be so much more determined to overcome his limitations, problems and enemies to improve the quality of his or her life. But the person who thinks this world will end will lack the necessary energy and drive to overcome in this world, because he or she expects Jesus to come back and to save them from their problems and hardship. Such a person will have an escapism mindset, but the other person will have an overcoming mindset. This explains the difference between a kingdom mindset and a Church mindset. Guess which is which!

So now we can clearly see according to Ephesians 3: 21 that the world we live in will never end. Now another question might be, what end is Jesus talking about? The answer is in the same verse - **throughout all ages, world without end**. This simply means this world has had different ages that have come and gone, and the age we live in, which is a Church age or grace age, will also come to an end. And when this age ends, we will then enter into a Kingdom age. I trust that we do understand now what Jesus meant when He said the end will come when the message of the Kingdom of God has been preached in all the world to all nations. The Church age will end and the kingdom age will come into the world with no end.

This means the end of the Church age will come when this message of the Kingdom of God has been preached in all the world for a witness to all nations. Therefore everyone will be able to witness the shift from the Church age to the Kingdom age. It will be dramatic because the message of the kingdom of God will produce a kingdom people in all the nations, and these kingdom people will rise to their rightful place, subduing the earth and having dominion over all the works of their Father's hands. All things will be put under their feet – there will be a definite separation and distinction between the Church and the World – watch it! Isaiah 9: 2 will be fulfilled in our very own eyes - *The people that walked in darkness have seen a great light: they that dwell in the land of the shadow of death, upon them hath the light shined.* And also Isaiah 60:2; *For, behold, the darkness shall cover the earth, and gross darkness the people: but the LORD shall arise upon thee, and his glory shall be seen upon thee.* The glory of the LORD shall be seen upon His people, not because of any other message that has been preached to produce such a witness to all nations, but because the message of the kingdom of God has been preached in all the world for a witness to all nations. **His Kingdom, His Power and His Glory will be seen upon us for a witness to all nations, because His Kingdom has fully come upon all the earth.**

And then we will also see this: *And the Gentiles shall come to thy light, and kings to the brightness of thy rising. Lift up thine eyes round about, and see: all they gather themselves together, they come to thee: thy sons shall come from far, and thy daughters shall be nursed at thy side. Then thou shalt see, and flow together, and thine heart shall fear, and be enlarged; because the abundance of the sea shall be converted unto thee, the forces of the Gentiles shall come unto thee. The multitude of camels shall cover thee, the dromedaries of Midian and Ephah; all they from Sheba shall come: they shall bring gold and incense; and they shall shew forth the* praises of the LORD. All the flocks of Kedar shall be gathered together unto thee, the rams of Nebaioth shall minister unto thee: they shall come up with acceptance on mine altar, and I will glorify the house of my glory. (Isaiah 60:3-7)

Where is the house of His glory? Is the Church not the house of His glory? Yes, we are the Church; therefore His glory will be seen upon us. The Church is not a building – we are His Temple. What? know ye not that your body is the temple of the Holy Ghost which is in you, which ye have of God, and ye are not your own? (1Corinthians 6:19) I hope you are getting excited, because we are a dwelling place of God in the Spirit - In whom all the building fitly framed together groweth unto an holy temple in the Lord: in whom ye also are builded together for an habitation of God through the Spirit. (Ephesians 2:21-22)

MISCONCEPTIONS REGARDING MATT 24: 5-12

Watch now very carefully as you read Matthew 24: 5-12 about all the terrible things that are about to happen in the world, for Jesus clearly says that these things will **not** usher in the end of the world. Yet many preach about these things, calling it the end-time message. Verse fourteen, on the other hand reveals what will usher in the end.

For many shall come in my name, saying, I am Christ; and shall deceive many. And ye shall hear of wars and rumours of wars: see that ye be not troubled: for all *these things* must come to pass, but the end is not yet. For nation shall rise against nation, and kingdom against kingdom: and there shall be famines, and pestilences, and earthquakes, in divers places. All these *are* the beginning of sorrows. Then shall they deliver you up to be afflicted, and shall kill you: and ye shall be hated of all nations for my name's sake. And then shall many be offended, and shall betray one another, and shall hate one another. And many false prophets shall rise,

and shall deceive many. **And because iniquity shall abound, the love of many shall wax cold.**

Let us now have a sober unemotional look at some of the things that have already happened, according to what Matthew 24: 5-12 talks about.

Matthew 24:5 For many shall come in my name, saying, I am Christ; and shall deceive many. Many have already come and gone in the name of the Lord and have already deceived many. This world is filled with deceived people who believe in a lie, accepting it as truth, sometimes because it sounds Christian-like. It may have the appearance and form of Christianity, but it actually denies the power of it. Having a form of godliness, but denying the power thereof: from such turn away. (2 Timothy 3:5)

It is very interesting to note that the Bible does not speak about a false Jesus or a false Lord. Why not? Because no man will ever be able to die on a cross for the sake of expressing their love for the world, accept Jesus. Secondly, no man can claim to be the ultimate Ruler of the entire world, accept our Lord Jesus – He alone is Lord! Yet, there are many false Christ's because many can perform deeds that remove burdens and yokes from people's lives even though the results may not be permanent. Christ simply means the anointing, which is the power of God, and it is this anointing that removes burdens and destroys yokes permanently.

Matthew 24: 6 And ye shall hear of wars and rumours of wars: see that ye be not troubled: for all these things must come to pass, __but the end is not yet__. Yes indeed, we have all heard and seen on television of wars and rumours of wars; so what? We should not be troubled about these things said Jesus. For all these things must come to pass. Believe me Jesus can be taken seriously on His word – He did say, but the end is not yet.

Matthew 24: 7 For nation shall rise against nation, and kingdom against kingdom: Many nations over the many years have stood up against one another. We thank God in South

Africa that we had a peaceful transition from the Apartheid era into the new democratic South Africa. Many other nations had blood-shed and never made a transition into a peaceful nation.

Matthew 24: 7b,8 and there shall be famines, and pestilences, and earthquakes, in divers places. All these are the beginning of sorrows. We have also witnessed famines, and pestilences (aids), and earthquakes, in divers places. Those who have never witnessed this might be those who do not watch television or who do not read the newspaper – good for them. Many so-called end-time preachers are using the media to develop their end-time sermons. Is it not written that we should not walk by sight, but by faith? We must preach what is in the Word, not what is happening in the world. Faith comes by hearing the Word; fear comes by hearing what is happening in the world. God has not given us a spirit of fear, but of power, love and a sound mind.

Matthew 24: 9 Then shall they deliver you up to be afflicted, and shall kill you: and ye shall be hated of all nations for my name's sake. Historical books about the dark ages tell of believers being delivered up to be afflicted and killed and being hated of all nations for the Lord's name. The disciples and their followers were persecuted by the Roman soldiers; the apostle Peter was crucified up side down for Jesus' name's sake; the Apostle John was cooked in a hot pot of oil; thousands of believers were killed, often in a terrible and inhumane way.

Matthew 24: 10 And then shall many be offended, and shall betray one another, and shall hate one another. Many of us who have been long enough in Church have seen how many believers have taken up an offense and never gotten over it and then eventually left the Church. Betrayal is not an uncommon thing to me and many others – I have been betrayed many times, but I have found it in my heart to forgive and to release those who have betrayed me. Moving on is more important to me than harbouring grudges and unforgiveness.

Matthew 24: 11 And many false prophets shall rise, and shall deceive many. Many false prophets have come and gone and have deceived many – thank God for the gift of discernment that has protected many of us from false prophets.

Matthew 24: 12 And because iniquity shall abound, the love of many shall wax cold. How many of us have not witnessed iniquity abounding, and been aware of love not being seen where it should be? Is it not cold-love to rape or kill a baby? Is it not cold-love to rape an elderly woman or kill an entire family or bomb a whole church building while the people are having Church? Is it not cold- love to come into a Church, a university, a school, and begin shooting left and right with machine-guns? How many of us have not witnessed a bank robbery and seen how innocent people are being terrorised and/or shot for the sake of money? (Television again.) And the newspapers are filled daily with terrible acts by people whose love has grown cold.

Everything Jesus spoke about in Matthew 24: 5-12 has already happened, but the end has not yet come, because Jesus clearly said in verse fourteen, the end will come when this gospel of the kingdom shall be preached in all the world for a witness unto all nations. The end will not yet come because at the moment, only a few preach the message of the kingdom of God. Let's continue to pray and trust the Lord that many other preachers will take up the message of the kingdom of God. Jesus clearly told his disciples what to preach when He sent them out - Go and preach, The Kingdom of heaven is near!' (Matthew 10:7)

The Prophet Samuel told King Saul that the LORD would have established his kingdom if he had only obeyed the LORD his God. The LORD will establish His kingdom in our lives and in the world, if the Church would obey Him preaching the message He has sent us to preach. As we move deeper into the times of the end, we will witness more disturbing things and troubling news as this world enters deeper into the birth pangs of the kingdom of God. These signs do not speak of the end, they speak of the imminent arrival of the kingdom of God – the end will come as we continue to preach the message of the kingdom.

THE DEVIL AND THE MESSAGE OF THE KINGDOM OF GOD.

Mark chapter 4 is a revelation of the devil's attitude towards the message of the kingdom of God. Nowhere else in scripture does it mention the devil coming for the word's sake. It is only recorded here in Mark 4 which explains the parable of the mystery of the kingdom of God. Jesus explained many other parables, but it was only when He spoke about the mystery of kingdom of God that the devil immediately came to take away the word that was sown, i.e.; the message of the kingdom of God. *And these are they by the way side, where the word is sown; but when they have heard, Satan cometh immediately, and taketh away the word that was sown in their hearts. (Mark 4:15)*

The devil is not threatened when we preach any other message, because no other message can produce a kingdom people. For as I stated earlier in this chapter, we become like the preaching and teaching we listen to. The devil is not threatened by principles that govern success, prosperity, wealth, riches, faith, healing, etc. But he **is** seriously threatened by kingdom principles, because kingdom principles produce kingdom citizens. The world is already filled with many people who are successful, prosperous and wealthy because *the children of this world are in their generation wiser than the children of light. (Luke 16:8)* In fact there are more wealthy people in the world than in the Church, and the interesting thing is, their wealth is laid up for the just for the establishment of the kingdom of God.

Let's get serious about the message of the kingdom of God and scare the hell out of the devil! I do not undermine any other teachings, because I have benefited greatly from the teachings of various great men of God in the Body of Christ. But just as the sons of Issachar had good understanding of the times and season to know what Israel ought to do, we too must get a clear understanding of the times and season to know what the Church ought to do in a time such as this. *And of the children of Issachar, which were men that had understanding of the times, to know what Israel ought to do. (1 Chronicles 12:32)*

This is the time and season for one unified message, which is the message of the Kingdom of God. This is the message that will bring an end to this current Church Age and usher in the Age of His Kingdom. This will be the outcome of having one language. *And the LORD will say, Behold, the Church is ONE, and they have all ONE language and ONE message; and this they begin to do: and now nothing will be restrained from them, which they have imagined to do. (Genesis 11:6)* Let's imagine seeing ourselves putting all things under our feet as we subdue the earth and exercise total dominion over all the works of our Father's hand. The original gods of this world will soon crush Satan (the god of this world) under their feet.

In conclusion: We understand that Pharaoh is a type of the devil and that everything in the Old Testament is a shadow of the REAL thing in the New Testament. With this understanding in mind how would we interpret Exodus 7:1 in the light of the New Testament Church? **And the LORD said unto Moses, See, I have made thee a god to Pharaoh.** We should also keep in mind that we were all made kings and priest unto our God. (Revelations 1:6) Therefore we can expect that the LORD will make all of His people a god to the devil. Remember the words of our Lord Jesus saying, *is it not written in your law, I said, you are gods? (John 10:34)* Let's go deeper as we look at Exodus 8:13 **and the LORD did according to the word of Moses.** Saints of God, we will enter into this dimension in God whereby God will make us gods to Satan, and the LORD will do according to the word of the saints. Why should we not have this kind of expectation? Is it not written that the New Testament is a better covenant than the Old Testament?; therefore we should have the expectation that God will exceed the works He has performed in the Old Testament.

For now we are in a war season just like King David was, but we too will enter a time of rest when the LORD will establish His kingdom through us, just as He has established His kingdom under the rulership of Solomon, and it was said of that time that there was no enemy in Israel. But why is it such a hard thing for Christians to believe that we too will enter a dimension of total rest in the LORD and that we too will be able to say that there is no devil in my life or in our land? We should continually be mindful that the OLD was and is a shadow, and we are the most privileged ones to experience the REAL thing. Already some of us can say this: 'There is no devil in my marriage; there is no devil in my family; there is no devil in my financial life; there is no devil in my relationships', etc. Hear me saints, we will be able to say this concerning all things that pertain to our lives if we build every aspect and facet of our lives upon kingdom principles. We have indeed received a kingdom that cannot be shaken!

Chapter Five

MANKIND'S TREASURE

Jesus likens the preciousness of the kingdom to treasure hid in a field; the which when a man hath found, he hideth, and for joy thereof goeth and selleth all that he hath, and buyeth that field. (Matthew 13:44) We are far more powerful than we think and experience in our ordinary lives. We have received a kingdom and we have been translated from the power of darkness into this glorious kingdom. Our Heavenly Father has been waiting a long time for the kingdom to be given back to His sons. Fear not, little flock; for it is your Father's good pleasure to give you the kingdom. (Luk 12:32) The kingdom has been brought nigh to us. Listen to what Jesus said to the multitudes in Luke 9: 27 while He was preaching to them. But I tell you of a truth, there be some standing here, which shall not taste of death, till they see the kingdom of God. We are heirs of the kingdom, (James 2:5) which means we have received the kingdom of God as our inheritance. The Father has qualified us through His Son, to be partakers of His inheritance in the saints in light. (Col 1: 12)

Just how willing are we to sell everything we have to come into the fullness of this kingdom that we have received through Jesus Christ? Can we make a similar connection like the man who found a treasure hidden in a field – do we connect with the reality that this kingdom which we have found is more precious than the treasure the man found in the field? The man sold everything he had to buy the field. Can we find it in our heart to give up everything we have for the sake of the kingdom?

GIVE UP TO GO UP!

Looking at what Jesus said in Luke 9:60 below, makes me realize that the kingdom demands our everything in order for us to experience the fullness of it and of everything God has in-store for us. It seems all different cultures in the world attach great value to the funeral of a loved one. In fact, funerals have become a huge enterprise because of the importance people attach to it. Jesus used such an event to challenge His disciples on their commitment regarding the kingdom of God. *Jesus said unto him, Let the dead bury their dead: but go thou and preach the kingdom of God.* (Luke 9:60) Reading this without a kingdom mindset might cause the reader to think that Jesus was a task master with no regard for the feelings of His followers. And then another disciple said this - *Lord, I will follow thee; but let me first go bid them farewell, which are at home at my house. And Jesus said unto him, No man, having put his hand to the plough, and looking back, is fit for the kingdom of God.* (Luke 9:61-62) The Message Bible puts verse 62 this way; **Jesus said, "No procrastination. No backward looks. You can't put God's kingdom off till tomorrow. Seize the day."**

- No procrastination
- No backward looks.
- Don't put God's kingdom off till tomorrow.
- Seize every moment of the day.

The opposite of this example is also very true – once a person gives himself completely to the advancement of the kingdom of God, he or she will never ever again procrastinate or look back, but instead such a person will have an abundance of energy to seize every given opportunity and will work endlessly without getting tired. Procrastination and looking back is what the kingdom of God will deliver a person from. The kingdom message imparts to us the habit of taking action, and everything we do becomes effortless. You will find yourself making the most of your time each and everyday. You will become a "do-it-now" person, and you will make your time serve you well.

So.....can we find it in our heart to give up everything we have for the sake of the kingdom? Does that mean we have to sell everything we have? Yes, but it is intangible things which are very precious to us that we need to let go of for the sake of the kingdom. The things we need to give up will be best understood by some of the other definitions of the kingdom of God. *A kingdom is a domain over which a king has rulership* is one definition. Here following are three others: the Amplified Bible defines the kingdom as *'God's way of doing things and being right'*. (Luke 4:43b) This means if we do things God's way we will always be in right standing with God and with man. The kingdom of God also means *'righteousness and peace and joy in the Holy Ghost'*; (Romans 14:17) and lastly, the Kingdom of God can be defined as **'the rule of God'**.

THE KINGDOM OF GOD IS GOD'S WAY OF DOING THINGS AND BEING RIGHT.

This means we have to give up our own way of doing things to align ourselves to God's way, so we can live effectively in the kingdom of God. This is easier said than done. Our way of doing things is something that has become an integral part of our lives; therefore there is a painful price to be paid to make these changes. Our ways are a by-product of our thoughts; that's why Jesus said, 'repent for the kingdom of God is at hand.' Repent means to change the way we think or to think differently. Our thoughts precede our ways - *For My thoughts are not your* thoughts, neither are your ways My ways, saith the LORD. (Isaiah 55:8)

Many of our ways are not God's ways, because our thoughts are not naturally in alignment with God's thoughts. The price we have to pay is to submit ourselves to the process of renewing our minds with God's thoughts as recorded in the Bible. In fact, this process requires our very lives, because as man thinks, so is he. **(Mathew 24:14)** This means we have to give our very lives, because we are products of our thoughts.

The Apostle Paul understood this; therefore his exhortation to renew our minds comes after saying that we should present our bodies a living sacrifice, holy, acceptable unto God. This implies that trying to change our thought life without presenting our bodies a living sacrifice will be a vain exercise. I beseech you therefore, brethren, by the mercies of God, that ye present your bodies a living sacrifice, holy, acceptable unto God, which is your reasonable service. And be not conformed to this world: but be ye transformed by the renewing of your mind, that ye may prove what is that good, and acceptable, and perfect, will of God. (Romans 12:1-2)

Not giving ourselves completely to God will cause unnecessary inner struggles and wrestles whenever we hear a thought- provoking saying or a hard saying from the Bible. A person who is dead to SELF will undergo this process much more easily than a person who is too full of himself. We are being changed and transformed whenever we accept and embrace new Biblical truth. His truth should become our shield and buckler. How can we actually measure whether we are being changed and transformed? We measure our growth by our ability to prove to others through our lifestyle that the will of God is good, it is acceptable, and it is perfect. Obviously this verse also defines the will of God as having these three attributes, so therefore;

- Can I prove that my personal life is good and acceptable and perfect?
- Can I prove that my marriage is good, and acceptable, and perfect?
- Can I prove that my family life is good, and acceptable and perfect?
- Can I prove that my financial life is good, and acceptable and perfect?
- Can I prove that my relationships are good, and acceptable and perfect?
- Can I prove that my testimony in my workplace is good, and acceptable and perfect?
- Can I prove that my testimony in my community is good, and acceptable and perfect?
- Can I prove that my ministry life is good, acceptable and perfect?
- Can I prove and that my thought life is good, and acceptable and perfect?
- Can I prove that my emotional life is good, and acceptable and perfect?
- Can I prove the will of God regarding the upbringing of our children?
- Can I prove that my prayer life is good, and acceptable and perfect?
- Can I prove that my WORD life is good, and acceptable and perfect?
- Can I prove that my relationship with the Father is good, and acceptable and perfect?
- And so I can go on and on...

Any area of our life that we can not yet prove is good and acceptable and perfect to others, is areas we need to bring into alignment with God's thoughts, which will automatically bring us into the will of God. Also notice that the areas where we can not yet prove the will of God are normally areas we might experience much hardship, problems, difficulties and tribulation, which is why Paul exhorted the disciples in Derbe saying, *we must through much tribulation enter into the kingdom of God.* (Acts 14:22) The renewing of our minds is God's way of bringing us into the fullness of His kingdom. This explains the other definition of the kingdom of God, which is the **rule of God.** We are effective in the kingdom of God when we are under His rule and honor His word regarding all things that pertain to our lives. God Almighty desires that every aspect of our lives should be brought into His glorious kingdom. This reminds me of the tussle between Moses and Pharaoh - *And Pharaoh called unto Moses, and said, Go ye, serve the LORD; only let your flocks and your herds be stayed: let your little ones also go with you. And Moses replied - Our cattle also shall go with us; there shall not a hoof be left behind; for thereof must we take to serve the LORD our God; and we know not with what we must serve the LORD, until we come thither.* (Exodus 10:26)

This should be our heartbeat – we should not leave anything concerning our lives outside the kingdom of God. Jesus said many times that the kingdom of God is like a seed, it is growing all the time; therefore we can be confident that everything about our lives will grow, multiply, increase and blossom when it is in the kingdom of God. The kingdom of God is the most fruitful place in all the earth.

THE KINGDOM OF GOD IS RIGHTEOUSNESS, PEACE AND JOY IN THE HOLY GHOST.

For the kingdom of God is not meat and drink; but righteousness, and peace, and joy in the Holy Ghost. (Romans 14:17) Where is the kingdom of God, according to this verse? The kingdom of God is in the Spirit; therefore the kingdom can only be experienced and established by those who walk not after the flesh, but after the Spirit. For those who are led by the Spirit of God are sons of God – therefore the kingdom of God will be established by the sons of God. *For the earnest expectation of the creature waiteth for the manifestation of the sons of God.* (Romans 8:19)

Even the earth longs for the establishment of the kingdom of God upon it; how much more do the hearts of humanity long for its establishment. If we walk after the flesh we cannot fully experience kingdom life, which is righteousness and peace and joy in the Holy Ghost. Righteousness, peace and joy are the fruit of the Spirit, and without righteousness we cannot enter the kingdom of heaven. *For I say unto you, That except your righteousness shall exceed the righteousness of the scribes and Pharisees, ye shall in no case enter into the kingdom of heaven.* (Matthew 5:20)

Righteousness is a gift from God just like the kingdom – we do not work to become righteous, neither do we work to get into the kingdom of God. Both gifts require us to submit to the Lordship of the King of the kingdom to receive His precious gifts. We become righteous by believing and receiving Jesus Christ as our Lord and Saviour. *For He (God) hath made Him (Jesus) to be sin for us, who knew no sin; that we might be made the righteousness of God in him.* (2 Corinthians 5:21) We became righteous because we believed in Jesus, nothing more and nothing less. This state of righteousness must also be fully experienced or translated into our day-to-day life experiences through our decision-making. Therefore if we make decisions that do not put us in right standing with God, we will not experience peace and joy in the Holy Ghost. Our decision-making should be WORD-based in order for us to be in right standing with God, with men and with His creation.

Creation itself is in great bondage of corruption, because of unrighteous people who made unrighteous decisions, affecting creation negatively. Therefore the earth has an earnest expectation for the manifestation of the sons of God, in the hope that their righteousness shall deliver it from its bondage, into the glorious liberty of the children of God. *Because the creature itself also shall be delivered from the bondage of corruption into the glorious liberty of the children of God (Romans 8:21)* Righteousness is more than being in right standing with God; we cannot be in right standing with God if we are not in right standing with our brothers and sisters, and the earth which God has given to the children of men. We have a responsibility towards God's creation. Bondage and corruption are by-products of unrighteousness, which causes a lack of peace and joy in the lives of humanity. This proves the need for the kingdom of God to be established so that there might be righteousness and peace and joy in the Holy Ghost upon all the earth.

A lack of peace, is a sign that we have made a decision that is not Word-based or righteous. We therefore pursue peace by making righteous WORD-based decisions, and in this way we can establish the kingdom of God; therefore joy is a sign that the kingdom of God has come upon whatever decision we have made. Let me therefore re-define righteousness in the light of this understanding: Righteousness is right standing with God, with man and with His creation; therefore we cannot be in right standing with man if we are not in right standing with God, and we cannot be in right standing with God if we are not in right standing with man. *If a man say, I love God, and hateth his brother, he is a liar: for he that loveth not his brother whom he hath seen, how can he love God whom he hath not seen? (1 John 4:20)*

GOD'S RULERSHIP

Proverbs 28:1b; but the righteous are bold as a lion. A lion is a ruler in the animal kingdom and righteous men are rulers in the kingdom of God. It is very important for us to root and ground ourselves in the word regarding our righteousness, which will produce a lion-like boldness in us, strengthening our God-given ability to rule in life.

It is also important to know and understand that a righteous man is not a man without sin; therefore sin cannot take away our righteousness. The Apostle John notes: if we say we have no sin, we deceive ourselves, and the truth is not in us, but if we do sin God is faithful and just to forgive us our sins, and to cleanse us from all unrighteousness, if we confess it. *And hath made us kings and priests unto God and his Father; to him be glory and dominion for ever and ever. Amen (Revelation 1:6)* The key word is "if" not "when" we sin, meaning we do not allow ourselves to become comfortable with sinning as we are no longer sinners, even though we may stumble and sin. Furthermore, we cannot rule if we allow the devil to make us feel condemned or guilty, as there is therefore no condemnation to them which are in Christ Jesus, who walk not after the flesh, but after the Spirit.

It is not possible to confess our sins when we are in the flesh; we confess our sins because we have been convicted by the Spirit and therefore, we align ourselves to our spirit-life through repentance. We must become immovable regarding our righteousness so our boldness can increase, which will in turn, increase our measure of rule. Let's hunger and thirst after righteousness – making righteous decisions regarding all things that pertain to life and godliness, so that the kingdom of God may be established through our every righteous decision and righteous action. *Blessed are they which do hunger and thirst after righteousness: for they shall be filled.* (Matthew 5:6)

We must all take up our responsibility to establish the kingdom of God. Religion has taught us that it is Jesus who will come to establish His kingdom. However a closer look at the 'kingdom' theme throughout scripture discounts this traditional mindset. Actually Jesus gave born again believers the kingdom. He gave us the mandate to establish His Father's rule upon the earth. His Father's rule is everything that is written in the Bible. 1Corinthians 15: 24 tells us what happens when Jesus comes; *Then cometh the end, when He shall have delivered up the kingdom to God, even the Father; when He shall have put down all rule and all authority.* This simply means Jesus will come to receive the kingdom from us which **we** have established, to deliver it up to God, even our Father. Jesus will then put or lay down all rule and authority that He has received from His Father. Jesus can not deliver the kingdom to God if the kingdom has not yet been established. *And Jesus came and spake unto them, saying, All power is given unto me in heaven and in earth.* (Matthew 28:18) Once Jesus has fulfilled His purpose with the rule and authority that the Father has given Him, He will then be able to lay rule and authority down. Their primary purpose was to enable Him to seek and save the lost kingdom and the sons of the kingdom. Then Jesus gave us the lost kingdom, and delegated to us His power and authority to establish it. *And Jesus came and spake unto them, saying, All power is given unto me in heaven and in earth. Go ye therefore, and teach all nations, baptizing them in the name of the Father, and of the Son, and of the Holy Ghost: Teaching them to observe all things whatsoever I have commanded you: and, lo, I am with you always, even unto the end of the world. Amen.* (Matthew 28:18-20) We tap into this delegated power and authority when we obey this great commission. Obedience is another word for responsibility.

The purpose of God cannot be fulfilled if we do not take up our responsibility in establishing it. There can be no authority without responsibility – we too can tap from the same rule and authority that Jesus had in order to fulfill His purpose on the earth, if we take up full responsibility for the establishment of the kingdom of God. The delegated power and authority that Jesus gave us are not less than the rule and authority that He had, because the same rule and authority that was needed to take back the kingdom from the devil, is needed to establish the kingdom. This is what the LORD said about the house of Ahaziah - *And the house of Ahaziah had no power to hold (keep; rule) the kingdom.* (2 Chronicles 22:9)

Let this never be said about us, the house of God, which is the Body of Christ. If we do not take up full responsibility for the kingdom of God, we too will have no power to rule or hold the kingdom. The power to rule the kingdom is closely related to us being responsible and accountable regarding it. Thus, taking up responsibility and being accountable is where authority comes from. Jesus has given us power and authority, but unless we are responsible we will not tap into our delegated power and authority; instead it will lie dormant.

Responsibility is a word that is made up of two words – response plus ability. Ability only kicks in when we fully respond positively to what is expected of us. Irresponsibility is the exact opposite, which is an inability to respond. We are unable to do something positive when we do not act on what is expected of us. Our response releases positive energy, which is the power to make something happen. A response is based on our knowledge of what is expected from us. Reaction is the negative form of response. Reaction is an emotionally charged decision. Our reaction therefore releases negative energy that cripples our ability to make something happen.

Many believers tend to react to all the bad news of what is happening in the world, causing them to be irresponsible with regards to their role in this troubled world. These kinds of believers tend to have an escapism mind-set, which is why the rapture teaching appeals to them. Well, there are some of us hearing all the bad news of world events and we feel burdened to establish the rule of God in our troubled world to make it a better place. Only those who take up this kind of full responsibility for the kingdom (that we have received), will enter into kingdom power and kingdom glory. 'Thy kingdom', 'Thy power' and 'Thy glory' is a progression. Responsibility is personal power and it precedes kingdom power and kingdom glory. God will not entrust us with kingdom power or glory, unless we prove ourselves faithful with personal power in the form of taking personal kingdom responsibility within ourselves.

Chapter Six

WHERE IS THE HOUSE OF GOD?

Preparing the Church for the GREAT escape is not a kingdom mindset, neither is it God's purpose for the Church, nor is it a planned event on His kingdom agenda. If it was so, Jesus would surely have made mention of the fact that His Father's plan is to rapture the Church out of the world. So why didn't He mention such a major event in the LIFE of the Church? Instead Jesus asked His Father not to take us (The Church) out of the world. *I pray not that Thou shouldest take them out of the world, but that thou shouldest keep them from the evil. (John 17:15)* The RAPTURE theory is a total contradiction to this prayer Jesus prayed; how dare we contradict Him and think it is fine. The rapture theory advocates that God will take the Church out of the world to be with Him. The rapture, according to those who preach its doctrine, is an escape from evil, but Jesus prayed to the Father to keep us from evil, not to escape from it. The Old Testament is filled with many examples of how God has always kept His people from evil.

On the other hand, the opposite of the rapture is very true – the Father desires to come down to be with us. *Jesus answered and said unto him, If a man love me, he will keep my words: and my Father will love him, and we will come unto him, and make our abode with him. (John 14:23)* The Message Bible puts it like this: *If anyone loves me, he will carefully* keep my word and my Father will love him - we'll move right into the neighborhood! The heart of the Father has always been to be among His people – it is religion that taught us that we will be raptured to be with God forever. It is not an easy task to speak contrary to what we have been taught for many years, but the truth remains that there is no direct scripture verse in the Bible promising us God will rapture His Church out of the world. On the contrary, Jesus prayed that the Father should not take us out of the world. Jesus also commanded us to pray for the kingdom of heaven to come down to earth, so that God's kingdom might be established **here**.

If we carefully read the main verse being used to explain the rapture doctrine, we will find that it does not directly speak about going to heaven. Let's rightly divide the word of God; Then we which are alive and remain shall be caught up together with them in the clouds, to meet the Lord in the air: and so shall we ever be with the Lord. (Thessalonians 4:17) **Any** interpretation of a single scripture verse must be closely related to what has been said in the entire chapter. One Thessalonians chapter four is an exhortation to charity, brotherly love, quiet industry, abstinence from undue sorrow for departed friends, for at Christ's coming all His saints shall be glorified. What exactly gives us the idea that we will go to heaven at Christ's return?

Conversely Jesus was very direct when He said, pray that the kingdom of heaven come down upon the earth as it is in heaven. The Bible makes no direct mention of going up, but it makes direct mention of heaven coming down; therefore one can conclude that we will meet the Lord in the air to be with Him on earth, because He is the King of kings (us) of the kingdom of God on the earth. Those of us who want to go up, don't want to grow up to rule the earth. Scripture speaks about **growing up** and not **going up**; therefore we should all have goals for growing up. Let us keep in mind that anything that is not in the Bible is not of God. Why would the LORD beat around the bush concerning the rapture concept and not states it directly in plain and simple words for everyone to understand, instead of leaving us at the mercy of man-made interpretations?

On the other hand, two verses in Exodus clearly state God wants to dwell among His people here on the earth. *And let them make me a sanctuary; that I may dwell among them. (Exodus 25:8) And I will dwell among the children of Israel, and I will be their God.* (Exodus 29:45) We Gentiles who have found the Lord Jesus Christ as our Saviour are now the people of God, and as such we represent Israel of old. Therefore God's original intention did not change, not at all. He is the same yesterday, today and forever. Putting the last scripture within our context: **And I will dwell among...** (My) **children....** (in My Church)**, and will be their God.**

Again I would like to emphasize the fact that without us taking responsibility for the kingdom of God, we will not have the power to rule the kingdom of God – there is no authority without responsibility. The RAPTURE is a very ill-prepared method for God's people to establish the kingdom of God; in fact, it teaches us to be irresponsible with the creation that God has given us. *The heaven, even the heavens, are the LORD'S: but the earth hath he given to the children of men. (Psalm 115:16)*

If we are to be raptured to be with God, why did Jesus teach us to pray for the kingdom of heaven to come? It would have made more sense if Jesus taught us to pray to go up to heaven – such a prayer would have supported the rapture theory very well. The verse above from Psalms makes it very clear that heaven is God's place, and there is no verse in the Bible contrary to this verse that supports the fact that God has made heaven to share it with His Church when He raptures them. Instead, God made the earth for His children and gave it to the children of men. It has been God's intention from the very beginning that men should rule the earth and that He Himself will rule in the heavenlies. In fact the Father's desire is for us to rule the earth exactly the way He is ruling the heavens. Heaven is perfect; therefore God wants the earth to become perfect under our rulership as we allow Him to perfect us.

It's like mum and dad – they have their own room and the children have theirs. Mum and dad have no intention for any of their children to move into their room. This is not a wow revelation; it is really easy to understand the Father's heart – why would we want to change this arrangement. Ultimately it is the devil who wants God's people to take their focus away from their kingdom mandate, which is to subdue the earth and to have dominion over all the works of their Father's hands.

What would you do as a father if you had given your son a piece of property to build a nice house for himself and his family, and then your son comes back to you after some time and tells you that thieves and robbers have kicked them off the property? Would this be your reply to your son: 'OK! It's fine my son, you and your family can come and stay with us.' Imagine you watch a movie of such an event. Don't you think the audience would be upset with such a reply from the son's father. So too, we have to stop being so churchy, allowing and accepting bad things happening to us without taking dominion. Our God is not a "nerd", The LORD is a man of war: the LORD is his name.... The LORD shall reign for ever and ever. (Exodus 15: 18) There is no way that the devil would ever be able to put our God into such a position of weakness. It happened once because of us – Jesus chose to become the innocent lamb slain for our sins, and the devil had the time of his life. It will not ever happen again, because He is no longer an innocent lamb – He is the LION of Judah. The lion hath roared, who will not fear? the Lord GOD hath spoken, who can but prophesy? (Amos 3:8)

The time has come for us to break away from old traditional mindsets concerning end-time events. In fact such teaching reduces the energy levels of believers. Let's open our hearts and begin to listen to what God has to say concerning His kingdom. For sure, there will be a dramatic increase in our energy levels.

The end time is not a scary thing; it will be the most glorious time in the life of the Church – this is what we have been waiting for.

HEAVEN IS GOD'S THRONE; IT IS NOT GOD'S HOUSE.

The early day believers ....*were more noble than those in Thessalonica, in that they received the word with all readiness of mind, and searched the Scriptures daily, whether those things were so.* (Acts 17:11) Unfortunately this is something that many of us neglect to do. This makes me realize how gullible I was in my early Christian days, because I received the word with all readiness of mind, but I did not search the Scriptures to see whether what I have been taught, was so. For example, we were taught that John 14: 2 meant Jesus is preparing mansions in heaven for us and that we will walk on streets of gold. Wow! That sounded very exciting and we could not wait to get to heaven. But a careful study of the word shows this is not so. *In my Father's house are many mansions: if it were not so, I would have told you. I go to prepare a place for you.*

I have searched the Scriptures diligently and discovered that nowhere in the Bible does the word say heaven is God's house. In fact the Scripture clearly says, heaven is God's throne. *But I say unto you, Swear not at all; neither by <u>heaven; for it is God's throne.</u>* (Matthew 5:34) Heaven is God's throne; heaven is not God's house. Also Revelation 22: 2 speaks about one street and not streets. I guess that one street must be the street that leads to the throne of God. It does not speak about streets with houses on both sides. *In the midst of the <u>street</u> of it, and on either side of the river, was there the tree of life, which bare twelve manner of fruits, and yielded her fruit every month: and the leaves of the tree were for the healing of the nations.* And the twelve gates were twelve pearls; every several gate was of one pearl: and <u>the **street** of the city</u> was pure gold, as it were transparent glass. And the twelve were twelve purls very several gate was of one pear and the street of the city was pure gold, as it were transparent glass (Revelation 21:21)

Let's consider the following scripture verses and allow the word to change our minds – that's what Jesus meant when He said, repent. Repent means to change the way we think about something. We should be quick to repent since the LORD Himself had a willingness to repent from an evil thought that He had towards the Israelites. And the LORD repented of the evil which he thought to do unto his people. (Exodus 32:14)

Psalm 11:4 The LORD is in his holy temple, the LORD's throne is in heaven: his eyes behold, his eyelids try, the children of men.

Psalm 103:19 The LORD hath prepared his throne in the heavens; and his kingdom ruleth over all.

Isaiah 66:1 Thus saith the LORD, The heaven is my throne, and the earth is my footstool: where is the house that ye build unto me? and where is the place of my rest?

The prophet Micaiah said this: 1Kings 22:19 And he said, Hear thou therefore the word of the LORD: I saw the LORD sitting on his throne, and all the host of heaven standing by him on his right hand and on his left.

Matthew 5:34 But I say unto you, Swear not at all; neither by heaven; for it is God's throne: Matthew 5:35 Nor by the earth; for it is his footstool: neither by Jerusalem; for it is the city of the great King.

The God we serve is a mind-blowing Awesome God – He is too BIG to be described in words. The heavens cannot contain Him; how much more can we contain Him upon the earth. But will God indeed dwell on the earth? behold, the heaven and heaven of heavens cannot contain thee; how much less this house that I have builded? (1Kings 8:27) The heavens is God's throne and the earth is God's footstool – it takes both places, heaven and earth to contain our God. He has to be in both places at the same time to be contained. Thus saith the LORD, The heaven is my throne, and the earth is my footstool. (Isaiah 66:1) I trust that we have established the TRUTH that heaven is not God's house; therefore John 14: 2 does not speak about houses being there. In my Father's house are many mansions: if it were not so, I would have told you. I go to prepare a place for you. Jesus did go to prepare a place for us; the preparation took place in heaven and _was the Father's house_ which has many mansions, but that house is now on earth – keeping in mind that we have established the TRUTH that heaven is not the Father's house. Please buy this truth and sell it not.

Was David in heaven when Jesus spoke about him entering the house of God? How he (David) entered into the house of God, and did eat the shewbread, which was not lawful for him to eat, neither for them which were with him, but only for the priesthood. (Matthew 12:24) No, David was not in heaven, Jesus was talking about an earthly temple which David had entered in to eat the shewbread. Let's also consider what Jesus said about His Father's house when He went into the temple in Jerusalem and cast out all those that sold and bought there. In His anger He threw over the tables of the moneychangers and the seats of them that sold doves. And said unto them, It is written, My house shall be called the house of prayer; but ye have made it a den of thieves. (Matthew 21:13) God's house is on the earth, therefore John 14:2 speaks about places that have been prepared for us in our Father's house (The Church). In my Father's house are many mansions: if it were not so, I would have told you. I go to prepare a place for you. That 'place' according to the Greek meaning speaks about locality; opportunities; room, position, etc. In other words Jesus was saying - in My Church is many opportunities and positions, ministry callings, assignments, mantles, mandates and projects that need to be carried out.

I also believe that Jacob's experience as recorded in Genesis 28: 16-17 was a prophetic picture of what the New Testament Church would experience. *And Jacob awaked out of his sleep, and he said, Surely the LORD is in this place; and I knew it not. And he was afraid, and said, How dreadful is this place! this is none other but the house of God, and this is the gate of heaven.* Jacob experienced God's manifested presence, just like we experience God in the Body of Christ in our Church services. And Jacob said, **this is the gate of heaven**. The Church is the gate of heaven, because the heaven and heaven of heavens cannot contain God. There is no separation between heaven and earth when God manifests Himself to His people. Let us truly connect with the Father's desire to dwell among His people. It is time to be real.

Chapter Seven

WHAT IS THE HOUSE OF GOD?

We see throughout scripture the three-dimensional unfolding of God's desire and plan to dwell among His people. God is three-dimensional and therefore He reveals Himself to us in a three dimensional facet. We know how God instructed Moses to build Him a tabernacle in accordance with the pattern He gave him. *And let them make me a sanctuary; that I may dwell among them. (Exodus 25:8)* Even the tabernacle was three-dimensional – outer court, Holy place and the Most Holy place. This tabernacle became obsolete when God instructed Solomon to build Him a temple, which was the second phase of the fulfillment of God's desire to dwell among His people. And the glory of the LORD filled the tabernacle of Moses and the temple of Solomon, because both men built according to God's pattern; therefore God came and dwelt among them as His glory filled the tabernacle and the temple. *And Moses was not able to enter into the tent of the congregation, because the cloud abode thereon, and the glory of the LORD filled the tabernacle. (Exodus 40:35)*

This very same thing happened when Solomon finished the temple of the LORD. *And it came to pass, when the priests were come out of the holy place, that the cloud filled the house of the LORD, So that the priests could not stand to minister because of the cloud: for the glory of the LORD had filled the* house of the LORD. Then spoke Solomon, The LORD said that he would dwell in the thick darkness. (1 Kings 8:10-11) And so Solomon's temple also became obsolete after it was broken down and destroyed, exactly as Jesus said. Jesus said to them, I am able to destroy the temple of God, and to re-build it in three days. This provoking statement was two-fold, because after many years the temple of Solomon was totally destroyed, but Jesus was also speaking of His own crucifixion and that on the third day He would be raised from death.

We can therefore clearly see that both the tabernacle of Moses and the temple of Solomon was a shadow of the true tabernacle which was Jesus Christ. And on one occasion Jesus, speaking of Himself, said to them: But I say unto you, That in this place is one greater than the temple. (Matthew 12:6) And when Jesus' flesh was ripped and torn apart on the cross.... behold, the veil of the temple was rent in twain from the top to the bottom; and the earth did quake, and the rocks rent. (Matthew 27:51) The crucifixion of Jesus brought in a new order, because there was no longer a separation between the Holy place and the Most Holy place when the veil of the temple was rent, and this has made the temple of Solomon obsolete. A new order which was the third phase of God's unfolding plan to dwell among His people had been introduced. In whom eye are also are builded together for an habitation of God through the Spirit. (Ephesians 2:22) The Hebrew writer defined this new order as a new and living way. By a new and living way, which he hath consecrated for us, through the veil, that is to say, His (Jesus') flesh, (Hebrews 10:20) we can now enter the Holy of Holies, which is the throne-room of God. We are covered by His blood; therefore the Father looks at us through the blood of Jesus, which makes us innocent in His sight. Let us therefore come boldly unto the throne of grace, that we may obtain mercy, and find grace to help in time of need. (Hebrews 4:16)

I am about to make a shocking statement based on this progressive unfolding of God's plan to dwell among His people. **We no longer have to follow the old order of approaching God from the outer court, into the Holy place and then into the Holies of Holies, because that order is no longer relevant in this dispensation of grace.** The old order was but a mere picture of the true tabernacle, which is Jesus Christ the hope of glory in us. The glory that was in the Holy of Holies at the mercy seat between the two cherubims is now in us. To whom God would make known what is the riches of the glory of this mystery among the Gentiles; which is Christ in you, the hope of glory: (Colossians 1:27) For God no longer dwells in temples made by hands – we are His dwelling place in the spirit. In whom ye also are builded together for a habitation of God through the Spirit. (Ephesians 2:22) Now we can completely understand why the Apostle Paul said; Know ye not that ye are the temple of God, and that the Spirit of God dwells in you. (1 Corinthians 3:16)

Therefore we can conclude that the place Jesus went to prepare for us when He returned to the Father was indeed the Church, which is the house of God. This 'place' was finally birthed on the day of Pentecost, when the believers were all filled with the Holy Ghost, and began to speak with other tongues, as the Spirit gave them utterance. And so the believers became the temple of God as the Holy Spirit indwelt them.

It was never the Father's intention to have a fixed place on the earth. A temple is far too limiting – God wants to be everywhere, anytime around everyone. Furthermore, this was only possible if He could be moved around by people in whom He could find a dwelling place. Hear what God said to David who had the desire to build Him a temple. Go and tell David my servant, Thus said the LORD, Thou shall not build me an house to dwell in: For I have not dwelt in an house since the day that I brought up Israel unto this day; but have gone from tent to tent, and from one tabernacle to another – (1Ch 17:4-5-6).

God was more pleased to move from tent to tent and from one tabernacle to another. He knew that the day would come that He is going to be moved around from nation to nation by born again believers who would be everywhere in the world. This makes perfect sense why Jesus said that it is best that I should go to the Father. Why was it best? Because Jesus could only be in one place at a time, but when the Spirit would come, He could be anywhere, any place and anytime in those who would receive Him?

But here is the crux of the matter - we have to seek for a balanced understanding, because a false balance is an abomination before the LORD. Just like Moses and Solomon had to build according to God's divine pattern to experience the fullness of God's glory, we too have to build according to God's pattern to experience the fullness of God's indwelling glory – Christ in us. Ephesians 2: 22 says we are being build together for a dwelling place or habitation of God through the Spirit. Yes, we are lively stones according to the Apostle Peter's writing. *Ye also, as lively stones, are built up a spiritual house, an holy priesthood, to offer up spiritual sacrifices, acceptable to God by Jesus Christ.* (1 Peter 2:5) There is also a divine pattern for the Church to follow to build up a spiritual house which will be acceptable to God by Jesus Christ. The glory of the LORD will cover the earth as the waters cover the sea, if we will follow the instructions of the divine pattern for the Church in the same way that Moses followed the divine pattern for the tabernacle and the way Solomon followed the divine pattern for the temple.

God Almighty has carried out His strategic plan through Moses, who built Him a tabernacle, and through Solomon, who built Him a temple, and finally, through Jesus Christ the true tabernacle of God, to dwell among His people and to be their God. God is now waiting on us, His Church to finish His SPIRITUAL HOUSE, so that He can pour out His glory, filling the entire earth with His Glory, Splendor and Awe, that all the nations may know that He is the only true and living God.

GOD'S DIVINE BUILDING PATTERN FOR THE CHURCH.

Bear with me as I repeat again that God is three-dimensional, (God the Father, God the Son and God the Holy Spirit) and His dealings with men will therefore always be three-dimensional since man himself is a three-dimensional (spirit-soul-body) being. The tabernacle of Moses and the temple of Solomon were also three-dimensional – outer court, Holy place and the Most Holy place. And God's strategic plan to dwell among His people has always been a three-dimensional plan – first the tabernacle of Moses, then the temple of Solomon and lastly Jesus Christ the true tabernacle of God. Therefore God's divine building pattern for the Church is also three-dimensional as we look at 1 Corinthians 12:28 **And God hath set some in the church, first apostles, secondarily prophets, thirdly teachers, after that miracles, then gifts of healings, helps, governments, diversities of tongues.**

GOD'S DIVINE PATTERN FOR THE CHURCH:

1. First apostles
2. Secondarily prophets
3. Thirdly teachers.

The Church in general, throughout the life span of the Church age, has not built according to the pattern as recorded in the verse above; therefore we cannot really experience what Moses and Solomon experienced when they had finished the tabernacle and the temple. And Moses was not able to enter into the tent of the congregation, because the cloud abode thereon, and the glory of the LORD filled the tabernacle. (Exodus 40:35) And it came to pass, when the priests were come out of the holy place, that the cloud filled the house of the LORD, so that the priests could not stand to minister because of the cloud: for the glory of the LORD had filled the house of the LORD. (1 Kings 8:10-11) We will also experience this, but in a greater dimension, because the new is better than the old and the latter will always be greater than the former. This will only happen if we build according to God's divine pattern like Moses and Solomon did.

We have all witnessed over the many years how the Church has put miracles, gifts of healing and helps ministries either first, second or third. This man-created disorder has attracted much criticism of miracles and healings from the world. But if the Church builds according to God's divine order – first apostles, secondarily prophets and thirdly teachers, we will experience greater miracles and healings and therefore a different response from the world. We will also experience God's favour and make a lasting impact upon the earth and all in it.

The miracles and healings that we have experienced thus far has been accomplished in the anointing dimension, but the Church is about to experience them in the **glory** dimension as we align ourselves to God's divine building pattern. It is very obvious according to the history of Israel, that a nation cannot be established by signs, wonders and miracles, because even though these were performed among the Israelites, they continued to fall in unbelief and doubt. Faith in God only comes by hearing the spoken word of God. Believe me saints, this messed up world will be sorted out and will be totally restored by the glory of God, just as God's glory fills the earth as the waters cover the sea. That all the people of the earth might know the hand of the LORD, that it is mighty: that ye might fear the LORD your God for ever. (Joshua 4:24)

Let's have a look at the purpose of this divine order and see why God has chosen three ministry gifts out of the five to be His divine building pattern. And He (Jesus) gave some, apostles; and some, prophets; and some, evangelists; and some, pastors and _teachers:_ (Ephesians 4:11) **Jesus** has chosen the apostles and prophets to lay the foundation of this spiritual house upon which we, the lively stones, will be built. _And are built upon the foundation of the apostles and prophets, Jesus Christ himself being the chief corner stone._ (Ephesians 4:20)

This foundation is the 'mysteries', which from the beginning of the world has been hidden in God, who created all things by Jesus Christ. _Even so then at this present time also there is a remnant according to the election of grace._ (Romans 11:5) The apostles and prophets have been graced by God to receive these deeper revelations and wisdom to lay the foundation of the house of God. _According to the grace of God which is given unto me, as a wise masterbuilder, I have laid the foundation, and another buildeth thereon. But let every man take heed how he buildeth thereupon._ (1 Corinthians 3:10)

The teacher has tremendous grace to explain these mysteries in easy understandable terms, so that all the saints will be united in their understanding concerning the knowledge of the Son of God. It is therefore important that the teacher ministry receives and accepts the ministry of the apostles and prophets, so they can then use their teaching gift to instruct the church with fresh and unfolding revelation.

The message the apostle and prophet brings, must be followed up and elaborated on by the teacher. The saints will not get the full picture of what God is saying until the teacher expounds, perhaps delivering many messages or teachings from one apostolic or prophetic message. The book of Numbers talks about the fact that God blows the trumpet once for the leaders, but twice for the people. This implies that a leader should receive the full picture first when the Word of God is shared by the apostle and the prophet; but the people will get it the second time around when the teacher teaches that word. The apostle Peter speaks about some of the things that the apostle Paul has written in his epistles, which are hard to understand by those who are unlearned and unstable. _As also in all his_ *epistles, speaking in them of these things; in which are some things hard to be understood, which they that are unlearned and unstable wrest, as they do also the other scriptures, unto their own destruction. (2 Peter 3:16)*

It therefore makes perfect sense to convert all the hard sayings of the prophets and apostles into softer sayings for the people. This is the role of the teacher. Keep in mind that foundation work is the hard and rough part of the process. Laying a foundation for a natural building construction confirms this truth.

WHAT MAKES A SAYING HARD?

A saying is hard when it contradicts our doctrine, tradition and belief system. Throughout the four gospels we read of many accounts of how the Sadducees (sad-to-see) and Pharisees (far-to-see) had been offended by Jesus' hard sayings. This very same thing is happening today in the Body of Christ. Much of what has been taught in the Church is now being challenged by the prophets and apostles since the Prophetic was only restored in the Body of Christ during the 1980's and the Apostolic during the 1990's. Before these decades, doctrine had been taught by men who did not have the understanding and grace to teach about the things they did. Sorry to say, this had to be corrected to bring the Church back into God's divine order. This correction came out as hard sayings to the people; therefore many saints have become critical and negative concerning the prophetic and the apostolic movement. But God is now releasing teachers who have been discipled and fathered by prophets and apostles to make these hard sayings clearer and more acceptable to the people.

We can therefore conclude that the apostles and prophets lay the foundation, and the teachers erect the walls of the building as they teach the word of God precept upon precept, line upon line, here a little and there a little. This spiritual house cannot be completed unless we build according to God's prescribed building pattern. The evangelist brings in the living stones (souls) and the pastor cleans up the stones, making them smooth and ready to be built together for a dwelling place of God in the Spirit. The beauty about this spiritual house is the fact that it does not need a roof, because SHE lives under an open heaven. Surely the house of God is the gate of heaven.

Let's now look at the purpose of the five-fold ministry: apostles, prophets, evangelist, pastors and teachers. The apostles must equip the saints, so that all the saints can do the work of an apostle; the prophets must equip the saints, so that all the saints can do the work of a prophet; the evangelists must equip the saints, so that all the saints can do the work of an evangelist (bringing in the living stones); and the pastors must equip the saints, so that all the saints can be good shepherds; the teachers must equip the saints, so that all the saints can teach the word of God accurately.

Jesus the true tabernacle of God was all of this – He did the work of the apostle, prophet, evangelist, pastor and teacher. We are predestined to be like Jesus, so that Jesus can be the first among many brethren. Because the creature itself also shall be delivered from the bondage of corruption into the glorious liberty of the children of God. (Romans 8:21)

The Hebrew writer says, He is not ashamed to call us His brethren. For both he that sanctifieth and they who are sanctified are all of one: for which cause he is not ashamed to call them brethren, (Hebrews 2:11) These five ministry gifts must function together as a team, because as individuals we cannot finish the task at hand, which is to build God a house.

WHEN WILL THE HOUSE OF GOD EVER BE FINISHED?

Jesus Christ is the true tabernacle of God; therefore we should all become like Him. The house of God will be finished when the following things have been accomplished by us building according to the divine plan in 1Corinthians 12: 28 when:

- All five ministry gifts work together as a team to equip the saints – no more superstars.
- All the saints are actively involved in ministry work – no more pew warmers.
- The Body of Christ are edified because all the saints are actively involved in ministry work, serving each other in humility and the fear of the LORD.
- There is unity of the faith in the Body, with all of us being fruitful and productive, building HER up, with no more time for unnecessary disagreements, idle babbling and busybodies, speaking things which we ought not.
- We all grow together in the knowledge of the Son of God, knowing what we ought to be like – keeping in mind that we become what we think about. *Till we all come in the unity of the faith, and of the knowledge of the Son of God, unto a perfect man, unto the measure of the stature of the fulness of Chris (Ephesians 4:13)*
- We become a perfect man, unto the measure of the stature of the fullness of Christ, the first born among many. **This is the PERFECT picture of the true tabernacle of God – the house of God.**

Chapter Eight

THE GLORY OF GOD

But as truly as I live, all the earth shall be filled with the glory of the LORD (Numbers 14: 21).

And the glory of the LORD shall be revealed, and all flesh shall see it together: for the mouth of the LORD hath spoken it (Isaiah 40: 5).

We must be confident about this one thing: God will finish what He started on the day of Pentecost – His Awesome glorious house will be completed on the earth for His name's sake, and for the sake of His kingdom and His people. Then, we too will experience what Moses and Solomon experienced with the completion of the Tabernacle of Moses and the temple of Solomon, but in a far greater dimension, because the latter house will be greater than the former house. And Moses was not able to enter into the tent of the congregation, because the cloud abode thereon, and the glory of the LORD filled the tabernacle. (Exodus 40:35) And also the temple of Solomon. And it came to pass, when the priests were come out of the holy place, that the cloud filled the house of the LORD, So that the priests could not stand to minister because of the cloud: for the glory of the LORD had filled the house of the LORD. Then spake Solomon, The LORD said that he would dwell in the thick darkness. (1 Kings 8:10-11)

It is time to believe what has been preached regarding the apostolic order and the need for the Church to build in accordance to God's divine building pattern. Many books have been written about the apostolic, many have heard the apostolic message and many are beginning to align themselves with it, rolling up their sleeves to build the house of God according to God's pattern and instructions. We cannot prolong this outcome with unbelief and negative talk about the Church. At the same time we should also be mindful that there are places in the nations that still need to hear the message regarding God's instructions to build according to His divine pattern.

Just as history has recorded the glory of the Tabernacle and the glory of the Temple, so also will history record the glory of the Church. It will be said of the Church: **And the saints of God were not able to enter into the house of God, because the cloud of His glory filled the house of God (The Church) and the saints could not minister because of the cloud: for the glory of the LORD had filled the house of God.** This corporate experience will dramatically restore, change and transform the saints of God from glory to glory, which will be a fulfillment of the prophetic psalm David wrote; and hast crowned him (man) with glory and honor. (Psalm 8:5)

Did Jesus not say, if we would believe, we would see the glory of God? Jesus saith unto her, Said I not unto thee, that, if thou wouldest believe, thou shouldest see the glory of God? (John 11:40) He said this in relation to the raising to life of Lazarus, whose dead state can be likened to the condition of the Church in many places. Christ is the hope of glory in us, but the time has come for us to go beyond hope, which is just an expectation; and to start entering into the faith realm regarding the glory of God in us. Faith is the substance of things hoped for - we have hoped for glory for many years. It is our faith in the glory of God in us that will cause it be manifested. Jesus Himself said to the Father – the glory which Thou gavest me I have given to them; that they may be one, even as we are one.

(John 17:22) Jesus has already given us the glory that the Father gave Him – Christ in us is our assurance of the glory that Jesus has given us. What are we waiting for? It is time to believe that the glory of God is in us and it is time to develop absolute faith in this powerful truth.

Unity is not an issue or our goal; unity will be a by-product of the manifested glory of God. Jesus said He has given us His glory, so that we may be one, just as the Father, Son and Holy Spirit are one. It is the glory of God that will produce oneness among all believers. This type of oneness we have failed to produce with our many man-made unity movements. Jesus clearly informed us how unity will come – He said the glory He had which the Father has given us, will make us become one. Jesus never instructed us to work on unity; therefore attempts to work on unity always have a reverse effect, because the flesh counts for nothing.

WE ARE DESTINED TO EXPERIENCE THE AWESOME GLORY OF GOD.

There is a great misunderstanding the enemy has sown into the hearts of believers regarding the glory of God that has hindered us from going beyond the hope of glory, to enter into faith for the glory of God. I will address this misunderstanding so that we may step into this faith realm, because unless we believe, we will not see His glory. We have had a false humility not to pursue the glory of God, which has the awesome weight and power to produce miraculous unity in the Church. Instead we have pursued unity, and failed desperately in all our attempts. We have indeed misunderstood Isaiah 48:10,11; *Behold, I have refined thee, but not with silver; I have chosen thee in the furnace of affliction. For mine own sake, even for mine own sake, will I do it: for how should my name be polluted? and I will not give my glory unto another.* We are being refined in the furnace of affliction, because that is what it takes for the glory of God to be released from within us. 2 Corinthians 4: 17 clarify the purpose of affliction as being a necessity for glory to be squeezed out of us. *For our light affliction, which is but for a moment, worketh for us a far more exceeding and eternal weight of glory*. Affliction works for us even though it feels like it is working against us at the time. The LORD enlarges us during times of affliction and distress to make room for more of His glory....*thou hast enlarged me when I was in distress,..* (Psalm 4:1)

God is saying to us in Isaiah 48: 11 that His name will be polluted or dishonored, if He does not prepare His people for His glory to be revealed through them. Yes, God is saying He will do it for His own sake, even for His own sake. Have you ever noticed the beauty of the LORD and the brightness of His glory on your countenance whenever you have come out of a time of affliction? If not, please let me encourage you to not be ignorant of what the LORD is doing in you when you are going through temporary light affliction. This is the part that many of us misunderstand - **I** (God) **will not give my glory unto another.** The Good News Bible puts it like this **what I do is done for my own sake--- I will not let my name be dishonored or let anyone else share the glory that should be mine and mine alone.**

Religion has taught us that we have no right to share in the glory of God, because the LORD will not let anyone else share in His glory. This lie has robbed us from trusting and believing God to share His glory with us, therefore we have never developed faith for glory. We have become stuck in our hope for glory – Christ in us. Let us therefore rightly divide this truth and see what God meant when He said, He will not give His glory to another, nor will He let anyone else share it with Him. Who is this 'anyone else' or 'another' that Isaiah 48 speaks about.

Let us first establish the fact that we are not 'another' or 'anyone else'. We are His very own blood washed people. *But* as many as received him, to them gave he power to become the sons of God, even to them that believe on his name. (John 1:12) We are therefore His offspring, and according to Acts 17: 28; ...in Him we live, and move, and have our being: He has created us in His image and likeness; therefore we are not another nor anyone else. Our lives are hidden in Him, and we are complete in Him, who is the head of all principality and power. He will not share His glory with just anyone, but He will share His glory with His own children – those who have received His Son. Also consider the fact that Jesus Himself has made us kings and priests unto our God and Father. There is no king without glory. This in fact is the hope of His calling to bring many sons unto glory. The words that Jesus spoke in John 17: 22 are worth repeating - the glory which You gave me I have given to them (us); that they may be one, even as we are one. And For we are members of his body, of his flesh, and of his bones; (Ephesians 5:30) therefore we will and are to share in His glory.

There is therefore no reason for us not to pursue the glory of God, because the Father will be glorified when we are being glorified. Whom He justified, them He also glorified. (Romans 8:30) We have all been justified by the blood of Jesus, therefore we will also be glorified. According to John 15: 4, Jesus is the vine and we are the branches. Which part of the plant bears the fruit or the glory of the flower? Is it not the branch? Jesus has no problem with us reflecting the beauty of His glory, but the branch will not bear fruit except it abide in the vine. It is religion that has a problem with believers being glorified. But as long as we abide in the vine (Jesus), we can all share in the glory of God. The heart of God can also be seen in the holy garments that were made for Aaron. And thou shalt make holy garments for Aaron thy brother for glory and for beauty. (Exodus 28:2) God Almighty desires above all things that His beauty and glory should be reflected by His people upon the face of the earth as a witness to all nations. Just have a look at Joseph's boldness regarding the glory that God gave him. *And ye shall tell my father of all my glory in Egypt, and of all that ye have seen; and ye shall haste and bring down my father hither. (Genesis 45:13)* Some will not be able to handle such a statement. Egypt or the world (market place) is the exact place where God wants His glory to shine through us, so that His name may be glorified and honoured among all the nations.

THE LORD WILL NOT SHARE HIS GLORY WITH ANOTHER OR ANYONE ELSE.

The reference of 'another or anyone else' was referring to Babylon and the Chaldean's. *But after that our fathers had provoked the God of heaven unto wrath, he gave them into the hand of Nebuchadnezzar the king of Babylon the Chaldean, who destroyed this house and carried the people away into Babylon. (Ezra 5:12)* God made it very clear that He will not share His glory with them. *And Babylon, the glory of kingdoms, the beauty of the Chaldees' excellency, shall be as when God overthrew Sodom and Gomorrah. (Isaiah 13:19)* We have to get real deep concerning this matter, so that we can fully understand why God said that He will not share His glory with them. Revelation 14: 8 calls Babylon a great city; therefore we can understand that greatness comes with much glory. That is why God said He will not share His glory with Babylon. It is therefore wise to ask what is it about Babylon that made her such a great city. To answer this question properly we first have to get an understanding of the true nature of glory.

For this reason we have to apply the principles of Biblical interpretation to get a clearer picture of glory. We will use the law of first mention, which says this: The meaning of a word where it is first mentioned, will maintain the same meaning and connotation throughout scripture if it is mentioned anywhere else in the Bible. The word glory is first mentioned in Genesis

31: 1 and it means 'wealth' in this specific context; therefore every time we see the word glory in the scriptures, it will have the meaning of wealth attached to it even though it also means something else in that specific verse or chapter. We will look at Genesis 30: 43; 31: 1 in two different Bible versions.

So Jacob's <u>wealth</u> was greatly increased; he had great flocks and women-servants and men-servants and camels and asses. .....Now it came to the ears of Jacob that Laban's sons were saying, Jacob has taken away all our father's property, and in this way he has got all this <u>wealth</u> (Bible in Basic English). (Genesis 31:1)

And the man increased exceedingly, and had much cattle, and maidservants, and menservants, and camels, and asses......And he heard the words of Laban's sons, saying, Jacob hath taken away all that was our father's; and of that which was our father's hath he gotten all this <u>glory</u> (King James Version Revised).

These two Bible versions clearly show the meaning of glory when it was first mentioned; ie. wealth is equal to glory. With this understanding we can now look at what made Babylon a great city. Babylon shared in the glory of God, because it was the wealthiest city on the earth. The prophet Isaiah prophesied about the day all the wealth and riches of Jerusalem would be carried into Babylon. Behold, the days come, that all that is in thine house, and that which thy fathers have laid up in store unto this day, shall be carried into Babylon: nothing shall be left, saith the LORD. (2 Kings 20:17) We see the fulfillment of this prophecy four chapters on; At that time the servants of Nebuchadnezzar king of Babylon came up against Jerusalem, and the city was besieged. (2Kings 24:10) All the wealth and riches that the Babylonians took from Jerusalem were added to all the wealth of the Egyptians when the king of Babylon took everything that pertained to the king of Egypt. And the king of Egypt came not again any more out of his land: for the king of Babylon had taken from the river of

Egypt unto the river Euphrates all that pertained to the king of Egypt. (2Kings 24:7)

Can you imagine the greatness and vastness of this wealth the Babylonians took from Jerusalem and Egypt? Egypt had great wealth, because there was a great wealth transference during a long season of famine under the leadership of Joseph. All the Egyptians in surrounding nations exchanged their possessions for food during the famine. God did not want to share His glory with Babylon, because the Babylonians were throwing their weight around with their arrogance and greatness. In our day and time Babylon speaks of the world's economic system, which dominates all other spheres of life – in other words, it runs all the world's systems. God has spoken, He will not share His glory. The prophet Haggai has prophesied God's action steps in this regard saying; And I will shake all nations, and the desire of all nations shall come: and I will fill this house with glory, saith the LORD of hosts. The silver is mine, and the gold is mine, saith the LORD of hosts. (Haggai 2:7-8) God has clearly defined the purpose of His wealth in Deuteronomy 8: 18. The purpose of wealth is to establish His covenant which He swore to our fathers, Abraham, Isaac and Jacob. It was a covenant of blessing so His people would be a blessing, then and now, to all nations. But instead, the wealth has ended up in the hands of the people God did not intend to share His glory with.

In these last days, wealth is not fulfilling its purpose because the majority of wealthy people do not belong to the house of God. This is why God promised in His word that He would transfer His wealth from the unrighteous to the righteous, so that wealth might fulfill its righteous purpose. And the wealth of the sinner is laid up for the just. (Proverbs 13:22) This wealth transference has already begun to take place as God begins to move more and more Christians into the market place. Many of us have been trained in Babylon in terms of how to set up and to run big companies and businesses, which are mere containers for wealth transference. Many others have been trained to set up schools, universities, colleges, hospitals and various training centers.

Saints of God, this is our time and season – it is the season when wealth is due to fulfill its purpose. We cannot be a blessing unless we are blessed with far more than enough. This brings us back to the purpose of the blessing as it was defined in the beginning. God blessed Adam and Eve, so that they could be **fruitful, multiply, replenish and subdue** the earth, and have total **dominion** over all the works of God's hands. By the way, God has not changed His mind; therefore He is mightily at work to position His Church for massive wealth transference. The people who know and understand this have no desire to be raptured; instead they desire long life, because the real game has just started.

Can you imagine being able to go into poverty stricken nations to set up schools and hospitals, etc.? How are you being affected seeing Oprah setting up schools in different nations and improving life standards and the quality of human life? Can you imagine setting up businesses in places where there are no jobs? Scripture is clear about the destiny of the Church and the destiny of Babylon.

BABYLON'S DESTINY: And there followed another angel, saying, Babylon is fallen, is fallen, that great city, because she made all nations drink of the wine of the wrath of her fornication. Revelation 14:8

THE CHURCH'S DESTINY: And the seventh angel sounded; and there were great voices in heaven, saying, The kingdoms of this world are become the kingdoms of our Lord, and of His Christ (The Body of Christ – the Church); and he shall reign forever and ever. Revelation 11:15

Let us consider this thing a done deal – the LORD our God will not share His glory with the world; therefore all the wealth in this world will eventually come back to the people of God. But ye shall be named the Priests of the LORD: men shall call you the Ministers of our God: ye shall eat the riches of the Gentiles, <u>and in their glory shall ye boast yourselves</u>. For your shame ye shall have double; and for confusion they shall rejoice in their portion: therefore in their land they shall possess the double: everlasting joy shall be unto them. (Isaiah 61:6-7) Their glory is their wealth; therefore we shall boast in their glory.

King David said, in Psalm 27: 13, he would have fainted (given up), unless he had believed to see the goodness of the LORD in the land of the living. I believe we can learn from this experience of David. We will surely faint unless we believe that we will see the glory of God. We have been hoping for the glory of God for many many years. Therefore we have need for the LORD to strengthen our hearts, because a deferred hope makes the heart sick. In the following verse David advices us what to do to overcome hopelessness. See the Good News Bible - Trust in the LORD. Have faith, do not despair. Trust in the LORD. And the King James Version - Wait on the LORD: be of good courage, and he shall strengthen thine heart: wait, I say, on the LORD.

The anointing dimension, in which the Church has been operating thus far is not enough to deal with the multitude of problems in the world – we desperately need the glory dimension. The anointing has done great and mighty works to heal and restore the saints of God, but it is not enough to restore the dying world we live in. It is the glory dimension that will position the Church to establish the kingdom of God upon the earth. King David testified; unless I have believed I would have not seen the goodness of the LORD in the land of living. (Psalm 27:13) And we can read this in the light of what God said to Moses when Moses asked the LORD to show him His glory; And he said, I beseech thee, shew me Thy glory. And he said, I will make all my goodness pass before thee, and I will proclaim the name of the LORD before thee; and will be gracious to whom I will be gracious, and will shew mercy on whom I will shew mercy. (Exodus 33:18)

This is the conclusion of the matter – David said, unless he had believed he would not have seen the glory of the LORD in the land of living. The glory of the LORD is the goodness of the LORD that makes us great. Let's go beyond the hope for glory, and let us **believe** that we will see the glory of the LORD in the land of the living. We develop this kind of faith exactly the same way we have developed faith for any other thing in God.

In conclusion: The LORD GOD ALMIGHTY is also very active in transferring great wealth into Aid Organisations which are committed to true good works and the spread of the gospel. For example, when the tsunami happened in Indonesia, billions of dollars were poured into aid organisations, some of which have a discreet but determined agenda to lead people to the Lord. **Thy kingdom, Thy power and Thy glory.**

Chapter Nine

AS IN THE DAYS OF NOAH

For too long we have shifted everything that sounds too good to be true, into a far away future. We think of ruling and reigning as something that will only happen after Jesus' return. Romans 5: 17 speaks of reigning in life right now, but so many Christians struggle to believe that there is also a promised land for them. James 2: 5 says we are heirs of this land, which is the kingdom of God, and according to Matthew 25: 34, it was prepared for us before the foundation of the earth. In the old Testament the majority of the Israelites who did not believe the promise, could not enter the land as they considered the giants in the land; we too are making the very same mistake in the name of the rapture - we are watching and reading the world 's bad news and making this our focus, not considering the fact that we have already overcome the world, according to 1John 5: 4-5. It reads like this: For whatsoever is born of God overcometh the world: and this is the victory that overcometh the world, even our faith. Who is he that overcometh the world, but he that believeth that Jesus is the Son of God?

So we are busy considering the many giants in the land, our fears backed up by preachers preaching bad news, instead of the good news of the kingdom of God. We are considering the giants of crime, giants of divorce, giants of aids, giants of abortion, gaints of banning prayer from schools, giants of wars and rumors of war etc, and speak of these things as the signs of the end-time. In fact, these troubling situations speak of the absence of an established kingdom - a kingdom of righteousness, peace and joy in the Holy Ghost. We should look at all these giants and have Caleb's mindset instead of having a rapture mindset. *And Caleb stilled the people before Moses, and said, Let us go up at once, and possess it; for we are well able to overcome it.* (Numbers 13:30)

You and I are well able to establish the kingdom of God! Why would God create the earth to give it to His children as their inheritance and then decide to give it to the devil and his foes, rapturing us to protect us from our enemies? This surely does not make any business sense – it only makes sense to a religious fearful mind, and explains why Jesus said the following words to the religious people of His time: *Thus have ye made the commandment of God of none effect by your tradition.* (Matthew 15:6) Tradition makes people mindless and ineffective. Please don't be one of them. These bad-news preachers are acting exactly like the spies who brought back an evil report to the camp of the Israelites. *And they brought up an evil report of the land which they had searched unto the children of Israel, saying, The land, through which we have gone to search it, is a land that eateth up the inhabitants thereof; and all the people that we saw in it are men of a great stature.* (Numbers 13:32)

How can we walk by faith if the Church makes bad news its focus, and we have no knowledge of what God is saying and doing in the midst of this troubled world? Is it not written that we should walk by faith and not by sight? Faith is based on His good news; fear is based on bad news - sight. The devil works openly; whereas our Father works in secret. Therefore, unless we enter the secret place of the Most high we will not know what God is saying and doing. Those of us who neglect to seek God will naturally focus on all the bad news coming their way. In fact, we don't have to seek for bad news because it will come to us via television or the newspaper. It is very true that sin is abounding upon the earth, and those of us who focus on this fact, continually listening to ongoing bad news and negative end-time teachings, will become faint hearted.

Many of us are too blind to see that *...where sin abounded, grace did much more abound.* (Romans 5:20) We will be either focusing on the grace of God that is abounding more and more, thus increasing our faith dramatically, or we will be focusing on sin abounding in the world, and thereby developing great fear. Our field of focus determines what we see and find in life. Whatever we focus on becomes a part of our lives. Jesus foreknew that sin would abound on the earth, therefore He posed this question: **shall I find faith on the earth with my second coming?** I tell you that he will avenge them speedily. *Nevertheless when the Son of man cometh, shall he find faith on the earth?* (Luke 18:8) This is the conclusion of the matter: Those of us who focus on the abounding grace of God will have faith when the Son of man comes. Those of us who focus on the abounding sin and all the bad news in the media will grow weak in faith and have none at His return.

These two opposing view-points surfaced in the Israelites during their time in the wilderness, splitting the people into two different camps. One camp had a willing mind to possess the promised land whilst the other camp was very fearful of the giants. Today these two different camps can be clearly seen emerging in the Church. There are those in the Church who preach the message of the kingdom of God saying, 'let's go up and possess the land'. On the other hand there is another camp that preaches the rapture, saying, 'we need to escape from this dangerous world, because our enemies are too big and we are like grasshoppers in their sight'. We need to ask ourselves - which camp am I in? There is no middle ground.

The current situation in the world is exactly as it was in the days of Noah. Sin abounded to such an extent that God could not take it anymore and decided to destroy all the wicked people from the earth. But where sin abounded, grace abounded more, and so Noah and his family were the only people who were positioned to receive the abounding grace of God. *But Noah found grace in the eyes of the LORD.* (Genesis 6:8) Today, as sin abounds in the earth, how many of us are positioning ourselves to receive the abounding grace that God is releasing upon mankind? Being more sin than grace-conscious results in us being totally dis-positioned.

Noah and his family were the remnant according to the election of grace in their day and time. *Even so then at this present time also there is a remnant according to the election of grace.* (Romans 11:5) We should never be deceived by what the majority is saying, because at **this** present time also, there is a remnant who believes the kingdom of God is their inheritance, and who don't put their hope in a rapture to escape all the trouble in the world. We are heirs of the kingdom which God promised to those who love Him. *For there is one God, and one mediator between God and men, the man Christ Jesus;* (1 Timothy 2:5) Kingdom-minded people are well aware of the fact that with an abundance of grace and the gift of righteousness they can fix all the trouble in the world, making it a better place.

WHO WILL BE TAKEN AWAY AND WHO WILL BE LEFT BEHIND?

Truly the Old Testament is but a shadow or type of the REAL thing, of which we, at this end of the age, are partakers. Thank God for the clear picture that the Old Testament paints for us. Jesus Himself gave us a clue as to how events will play out with the coming of the Son of man. He said, that His coming will be like the days of Noah; therefore we can only much more clearly understand how the coming of the Lord will be, by studying the flood of Noah and its after-effects.

The earth in the days of Noah was corrupt and filled with terrible violence, which is exactly what we are experiencing in the world today. *And GOD saw that the wickedness of man was great in the earth, and that every imagination of the thoughts of his heart was only evil continually. (Genesis 6:5) But as the days of Noah were, so shall also the coming of the Son of man be. For as in the days that were before the flood they were eating and drinking, marrying and giving in marriage, until the day that Noah entered into the ark. (Matthew 24:37-38)* Noah was in the world, but not of the world. He entered into the ark, which was a dimension beyond the seen world, as it represents the presence of God. Jesus Himself said, we are not of the world; *If ye were of the world, the world would love his own: but because ye are not of the world, but I have chosen you out of the world, therefore the world hateth you (John 15:19)* therefore the destruction that will come upon the earth will not affect us, just like it did not affect Noah and his family. But the flood came, and took all the unrighteous people away; so shall also the coming of the Son of man be. The unrighteous in our day and time will also be taken away from the earth just like in the days of Noah.

Psalm 37:28 is a prophetic picture of the future of the wicked and the saints of God - *For the LORD loveth judgment, and forsaketh not his saints; they are preserved for ever: but the seed of the wicked shall be cut off.* The seed of the wicked shall be cut off with the coming of the Son of man just like in the days of Noah. Noah and his family were not raptured or taken away; it was the wicked people that were removed from the earth. Noah and his family were left behind, which is a total contradiction of the rapture theory.

The rapture theory says the unrighteous will be left behind and the righteous people will be taken away. It was not so in the days of Noah; instead, the waters upon the earth increased, the ark was lifted above the earth, and the wicked were drowned in the flood covering the earth. Noah and his family were lifted high above all the nations of the earth – they were above and not beneath; they were the head and not the tail when the earth was shaken with a flood, because Noah and his family had hearkened diligently to the voice of the LORD their God. God did for Noah exactly what He promised the Israelites when He said; *And it shall come to pass, if thou shalt hearken diligently unto the voice of the LORD thy God, to observe and to do all his commandments which I command thee this day, that the LORD thy God will set thee on high above all nations of the earth. (Deuteronomy 28:1)*

Let's keep this in mind for those who reason by human understanding that the lifting up of the ark above the earth is a type of the rapture: it can not be so, considering Noah and his family were not in heaven with God! The rapture theory advocates that we will be raptured to be with God forever. However when the water dried up from the earth, Noah and his family had their feet planted firmly on the ground, and all the unrighteous were gone. *And every living substance was destroyed which was upon the face of the ground, both man, and cattle, and the creeping things, and the fowl of the heaven; and they were destroyed from the earth: and Noah only remained alive, and they that were with him in the ark . (Genesis 7:23)*

Jesus clearly said that this is exactly how things during the end of the world will play out when the Son of man returns. There will be no rapture; rather the righteous people will be left behind and the unrighteous will be taken away and be destroyed from the earth. The righteous will be left behind, because the earth has been given to the children of man. Jesus has spoken and so it will be. *And knew not until the flood came, and took them all away; so shall also the coming of the Son of man be. Then shall two be in the field; the one shall be taken, and the other left. Two women shall be grinding at the mill; the one shall be taken, and the other left. (Matthew 24:39-40)*

It is therefore so important for us to practice the presence of the LORD, so that we are not caught up in the things of the world when the Son of man returns. The presence of God is our protection just like the ark was Noah's protection. The presence of God is His secret place, protecting us from the destructive things that are happening in the world today. Even though we are in this world we are not of it. *He that dwelleth in the secret place of the most High shall abide under the shadow of the Almighty. I will say of the LORD, He is my refuge and my fortress: my God; in him will I trust. (Psalm 91:1-2)* We have all witnessed with the 11 September tragic event in New York how God protected blood-washed Christians. Many Christians whose lives were spared had remarkable testimonies of how God kept them in that hour.

THE REAL MESSAGE IS NOT TO GET SAVED TO GO TO HEAVEN – THE REAL MESSAGE IS TO GET SAVED, BE DELIVERED, BE HEALED, BE RENEWED IN YOUR MIND, BE RESTORED AND REFORMED, BE CHANGED AND TRANSFORMED TO RULE THE EARTH AS GOD'S REPRESENTATIVES.

The kingdom of God is not a democracy that says the majority rules. The majority may rule in our secular systems, but it is a remnant in the kingdom of God that will rule. *Even so then at this present time also there is a remnant according to the election of grace. (Romans 11:5)* Noah and his family were a remnant according to the election of grace in their day and time, because *Noah found grace in the eyes of the LORD. ... (He) was a just man and perfect in his generations, and Noah walked with God. (Genesis 6:8)* Noah reveals the qualities of a remnant according to the election of grace. Let's have a look at these qualities to examine ourselves:

- Did you find grace in the eyes of the LORD?
- Are you a just man or woman in your generation?
- Are you perfect or mature in your generation?
- Do you walk with God and do you have a close intimate relationship with God?

In a nutshell, the remnant according to the election of grace are those who have grown close to the LORD their God – this group has passed beyond an Outer Court experience and has come into the Holy Place where they have been sanctified and set apart from the world. But they do not stop right there; they enter into a Holy of Holies experience with God. They are coming daily into the throne of grace where they obtain mercy and find grace to help in time of need. This group of people can easily be noticed by their unselfish lifestyle, because they are change-agents. They are not needy, because they daily find grace to help themselves in their times of need; therefore they have what it takes to meet other people's needs.

They are the ones who have taken up the responsibility for the establishment of God's kingdom here on earth. Does this person sound like you or does it sound like some other unique believer whom you admire? Keep on keeping on, if this person sounds like you. The best is yet to come, because there is an abounding grace on the earth which will take us from a measure of grace, *But unto every one of us is given grace according to the measure of the gift of Christ (Ephesians 4:7)* to strong grace, *Thou therefore, my son, be strong in the grace that is in Christ Jesus (2Timothy 2:1.)* into an abundance of grace. *For if by one man's offence death reigned by one much more they which receive abundance of grace and of the gift of righteousness shall reign in life by one, Jesus Chris. (Romans 5:17)* An abundance of grace and the gift of righteousness will bring us into total rulership here on earth. The earth belongs to us; we are not those who desire to escape the earth to hand over our inheritance to Satan, like Adam and Eve did.

If this person is not you but someone whom you admire, let me say to you, it is not too late, not at all. It just means you have to draw closer to our Dad – He is waiting for you! He is saying to you come up higher my son or my daughter. Draw near to Me with a true heart in full assurance of faith, having your heart sprinkled from an evil conscience, and your body washed with pure water. His Word is pure water – Jesus said you are already cleansed by the spoken word. Submit yourself to the spoken word, let it sanctify you. Let go of all your selfish fleshly desires that distracts you from Him and learn to desire Him more than anything else. If we put Him first, He will give us all the desires of our heart. He wants to be the MOST important person in our lives.

THE MEEK SHALL INHERIT THE EARTH.

The kingdom of God is the earth and the fullness thereof, the world and they that dwell therein. Yes, the kingdom of God includes all the nations of the earth and the uttermost parts of the earth as our possession. All of this is our inheritance according to James 2: 5. This is far beyond what we could have ever imagined, asked or thought. No wonder the Apostle Paul describes our inheritance in this fashion: THE RICHES OF THE GLORY OF HIS INHERITANCE. Who on earth could have ever imagined having all the nations of the earth for their inheritance, and the uttermost parts of the earth for their possession *Ask of me, and I shall give thee the heathen for thine inheritance, and the uttermost parts of the earth for thy possession. (Psalm 2:8)* This is why we have the need for the eyes of our understanding to be enlightened, so that we may truly know what is the hope of His calling, and what are the riches of the glory of His inheritance in the saints? *The eyes of your understanding being enlightened; that ye may know what is the hope of his calling, and what the riches of the glory of his inheritance in the saints, (Ephesians 1:18)* The revelation of our inheritance spontaneously explodes into thanksgiving - the Father has qualified us to share in the inheritance of the holy ones in the light! *Giving thanks unto the Father, which hath made us meet to be partakers of the inheritance of the saints in light (Colossians 1:12)*

God in His great love and mercy invites all of us to be partakers of His inheritance. He resists the proud, but gives grace to the humble; therefore the meek will be the ones who will inherit the earth. I believe all of us have tasted the bitter taste of an arrogant person being in charge of something. Would you put such a person in charge if you had the power to appoint a person to an influential position? So why would God allow the proud and arrogant to inherit the earth?

The meek are God's chosen ones according to Psalm 37:11 - But the meek (gentle, humble, lowly) shall inherit the earth; and shall delight themselves in the abundance of peace. The LORD has given the earth to the children of men, but it will be the meek who will eventually inherit the earth. It is not about going to heaven, it is about inheriting the earth. Will you? Will I? Be one of these meek heirs.

LEARNING FROM THE MEEKEST MAN ON EARTH.

It is recorded in Numbers that Moses was the meekest man on earth. As usual, we all tend to want to learn from champions or the best. It therefore makes sense to learn from Moses what it really takes to be meek, since the earth will be inherited by the meek. Now the man Moses was very meek, above all the men which were upon the face of the earth. (Numbers 12:3)

Let us get this straight, meekness is not weakness. Meekness means strength and power under control; whereas pride is a display of strength and power. This is why God confounds the strong by displaying His strength through those who appear weak. He confounds the wise by displaying His wisdom through those who appear foolish. But God hath chosen the foolish things of the world to confound the wise; and God hath chosen the weak things of the world to confound the things which are mighty. (1Corintheans 1:27) God chose Moses (who was a weak stuttering fool in the eyes of Pharaoh) to confound the all powerful wise Pharaoh. Moses' weakness and foolishness qualified him to rule over the evil god (Pharaoh) of his day and time.

Of His communication with Moses, God had this to say; *With him* (Moses) *will I speak mouth to mouth, even apparently, and not in dark speeches.* (Numbers 12:8) *And there arose not a prophet since in Israel like unto Moses, whom the LORD knew face to face.* (Deuteronomy 34:10) This means that Moses did not have to interpret what God said to him. This was indeed a result of his meekness before God, but how did Moses produce such meekness? The answer to this question is found in Psalm 25:14; *The secret of the LORD is with them that fear him; and he will shew them his covenant.* God Almighty had a mouth to mouth conversation with Moses, because Moses feared God. The fear of the LORD produces hatred towards evil, pride and arrogance; therefore Moses had an inability to be prideful and arrogant because of the fear of the LORD that was at work in him. *The fear of the LORD is to hate evil: pride, and arrogance, and the evil way, and the froward mouth, do I hate.* (Proverbs 8:13)

The absence of pride and arrogance gives room to humility. The fear of the LORD is also the beginning of wisdom and the knowledge of God, which enhances intimacy and closeness with God. It is therefore obvious to conclude that Moses' fear of God was a direct result of his intimate encounter with God by the burning bush in the mountains. Intimacy with God is therefore vital for us to develop a deep reverential respectful fear for God, which will in turn produce a hatred in us for evil, pride and arrogance. This kind of hatred will produce a Godly meekness in us, preparing us to inherit the earth.

Chapter Ten

THE DESTINY OF THE SAINTS

Jesus was equally available to everyone during His earthly ministry. The woman who had five husbands and the woman who was caught in the act of adultery, both had a face to face encounter with Him, and both of their lives were dramatically impacted and changed by His presence and words. We have the power to choose how close we want to get to Jesus – there are no limits and no boundaries. We can choose to be like the multitudes who followed Him, or the hundred and twenty that drew closer to Him than the multitudes, or the seventy that were closer to Him than the hundred and twenty, or the twelve disciples who were even closer than the seventy, or the three disciples (John, Peter and James), who were closer still than the other disciples, or John, who listened to the Lord's heartbeat.

The tabernacle of Moses had a floor plan consisting of three areas; the outer court, the Holy place and the Most Holy place, and these areas illustrate to us today, in the most practical way, just how close we can truly get to the Father. The people in the outer court worshipped Him from afar; the priest who ministered in the Holy place had a Holy Ghost encounter; the high priest who ministered in the Most Holy place, had the most intimate glorious experience with God. Of course, today the tabernacle of Moses is obsolete, but our Christian life perfectly aligns with one of these three areas, according to our experience and commitment. Jesus is the true tabernacle, therefore His names, which represent His Character and nature, also represent these "three-dimensional-relational-levels". These three dimensions are recorded in Act 2:36 Therefore let all the house of Israel know assuredly, that God hath made that same Jesus, whom ye have crucified, both Lord and Christ. These are the three-dimensions: Jesus – Christ – Lord. Knowing Him as Jesus represents an outer court experience; knowing Him as Christ represents a Holy place experience; knowing Him as Lord represents a Holy of Holies experience.

THE OUTER COURT BELIEVERS

'Outer Court' believers are those who just go to Church on Sundays and do all the churchy stuff, returning back to their normal worldly lifestyle from Monday to Saturday. Can you see the absence of the fear of the LORD in these Christians? Evil, pride and arrogance can easily slip into our lives if there is no fear of the LORD. These believers have come to know Him as Jesus (the lamb of God), who died for our sins, saved us and washed us in His own blood. This kind of relationship is a one-sided-kind-of-relationship where only one person initiates and maintains the friendship. This kind of relationship does not go beyond an outer court experience (shallow experience), and until there is a giving of himself or herself, the relationship is doomed to break down. We do experience the presence of Jesus in the outer court, which gives us an awareness of Him; whereas people not yet born again have no awareness or consciousness of Jesus.

There is a barely discernible difference between an outer court believer and the people who are not saved. The only difference is the fact that an outer court believer had an experience with Jesus as their saviour, while the sinner has not yet met Jesus. It makes real sense that many outer court believers continually fall back into old sins and their old ways, because their past has not been removed by the power of God. Our freedom increases progressively as we travel the journey through to the Holy place or the Christ dimension as we walk with God on a day-to-day basis.

THE HOLY PLACE BELIEVERS

The Holy place disciples on the other hand, are the ones who have been convicted of their worldly ways and now serve the LORD with a greater commitment and a more serious focus. They are believers who have pressed beyond the outer court or Jesus dimension. This can only happen when we begin to give of ourselves in terms of our time, energy, and effort, setting aside our selfish and carnal desires and goals, and letting go of old relationships that do not support our new lifestyle, and of other conflicting interests; for the sake of our relationship with Him.

It is only when we do this that we can truly get to know Him as Christ. We make a transition from the outer court into the Holy place when we die to self. It is right here, where we get to know Jesus as the Christ. Here is a true message: "If we died with Christ, we will live with Him." (2 Timothy 2:1) We get saved in the Jesus dimension, but real change and transformation takes place in the Christ dimension. Therefore if any man be in Christ, he is a new creature: old things are passed away; behold, all things are become new. (2 Corinthians 5:17) Christ is not Jesus' second name or surname, it means the anointed One and His anointing, which is the power of God. It is the anointing that removes our past and makes all things becomes new. According to Isaiah 10:27, the anointing can also be defined as God's burden-removing, yoke-destroying power; And it shall come to pass in that day, that his (the enemy's) burden shall be taken away from off thy shoulder, and his yoke from off thy neck, and the yoke shall be destroyed because of the anointing.

Christ is the power of God according to 1Corinthians 1: 24. It is the anointing or the power of God that removes the burdens and yokes of our past, no one else can do it for us, we personally have to be sanctified in the Christ dimension, which is a Holy place experience. *But of him are ye in Christ Jesus, who of God is made unto us wisdom, and righteousness, and sanctification, and redemption. (1 Corinthians 1:30)* It is the anointing, the Christ dimension, the Holy place that sets us apart from the world.

The furniture pieces situated in the Holy place, speak of the things that enhances and develops our relationship with God. The table of shew bread speaks of our intimacy in the word of God. Jesus said, *man shall not live by bread alone, but by every word that proceedeth out of the mouth of God. (Matthew 4:4)* Time in the word is equal to time spent with God, because the word is God. *In the beginning was the Word, and the Word was with God, and the Word was God. (John 1:1)*

The seven-lamp candlestick speaks of our relationship with the Holy Spirit, because no one can come to the Father unless the Spirit draws them. Therefore just as the priest had to make sure that there was oil in the lamps, so also should we be filled with the Spirit of God on a day-to-day basis. *And be not drunk with wine, wherein is excess; but be filled with the Spirit. (Ephesians 5:18)* Praying in tongues is the most effective way to be continually filled with the Spirit.

The table of incense speaks of our prayer life, intercession and worship. *And the smoke of the incense, which came with the prayers of the saints, ascended up before God out of the angel's hand. (Revelation 8:4)*

- Seven candle stick – Life in the Spirit.
- Table of showbread – Life in the Word.
- Alter of incense – Prayer, praise and worship lifestyle.

It takes real discipline to maintain our lifestyle in the Christ dimension; therefore we can also say that the transition from the outer court or Jesus dimension into the Holy place or Christ dimension is also a transition from being a believer to a disciple of Jesus Christ. There is no real big deal in being a believer, because the devil himself is a believer - *Thou believest that there is one God; thou doest well: the devils also believe, and tremble.* (James 2:19) As we unfold this revelation we will see what the destiny of believers will be at the end. Becoming a true disciple of Jesus Christ, will put upon our lives a mark of meekness which says; *It is no longer I who live, but Christ who lives in me.* Each one of us must reach this dimension in Christ; keeping in mind that it is the meek that will inherit the earth. *I am crucified with Christ: nevertheless I live; yet not I, but Christ liveth in me: and the life which I now live in the flesh I live by the faith of the Son of God, who loved me, and gave himself for me.* (Galatians 2:20) This is not a verse to be quoted religiously; it must become a true life experience in order for us to say, 'I am crucified with Christ'. It is more than right for us to die for Him, because He died for us.

Our relationship with Him can only begin to grow when we also die for Him. Dying to self is an ongoing process and He will continue to shed light on areas He expects us to die in. We must continually decrease in order for Him to increase. Hear the heart of Jesus in these words - *And he that taketh not his cross, and followeth after Me, is not worthy of Me.* (Matthew 10:38) And; *He who has the desire to keep his life will have it taken from him, and he who gives up his life because of Me will have it given back to him.* (John 12:25)

The desire to keep our lives is a reflection of the value we place on the new life we have found in Jesus. This means we are still enjoying the kind of life we lived before we met Jesus. Jesus said if that is the case such a person's life will be taken from him. Those of us who find it in our hearts to give up our lives for Christ's sake, will find real life in Christ, which is a far superior kind of life.

THE MOST HOLY PLACE BELIEVERS

We will reign with Him, if we endure our walk with Him in the Christ dimension and its sanctification process. *If we go on to the end, then we will be ruling with Him. (2Timothy 2: 12)* Our walk in the Christ dimension seems like a never-ending process at times; therefore Apostle Paul exhorts us to keep pressing on to the end, as it culmulates in the third dimension. This is the Lord dimension, a dimension where we are ruling and reigning with Him. It is in this dimension that we experience the glory of God, which in the tabernacle, was found in the Most Holy place.

This dimension is for those who have made Him Lord in all areas of their lives, which is another mark of true meekness. This group is the meek or the remnant, who will inherit the earth. Is there total surrender to His Lordship in our lives? Which areas do we still like to have personal control over? There is such awe in this dimension, a growing awareness that it is not by might nor by power that we can accomplish anything in His kingdom, but only by the Spirit of God. Another thing that becomes so real is the fact that everything we would ever accomplish is a gift from God – it is by grace through faith and not of ourselves. We can only conquer in life, if we have allowed Him to conquer us. Our inner wrestles and struggles are mere signs of areas in our lives where we have not yet been conquered by the Lord. Let us continue to go on to the end until all areas of our lives are under His Lordship.

WHAT WILL BE THE DESTINY OF THOSE WHO DID NOT GO BEYOND THE OUTER COURT IN THEIR RELATIONSHIP WITH THE LORD?

Many of us have been deceived into thinking that getting saved qualifies us to go to heaven, which is far from the truth. Jesus clearly taught that it is not every one who says; 'Lord, Lord', shall enter into the kingdom of heaven. Not every one that said unto me, Lord, Lord, shall enter into the kingdom of heaven; but he that does the will of my Father which is in heaven. (Matthew 7:21) It is the will of God that we should all get to know His Son three-dimensionally, as Jesus, as Christ, and as Lord. Eternal life, according to John 17: 3 is to know the only true God and Jesus Christ whom God has sent. Those who know Him personally as Jesus, as Christ and as Lord will come into their rightful places of ruling and reigning. But the people that do know their God (Jesus, Christ, Lord) shall be strong, and do exploits. (Daniel 11:32)

It is not our works that give us access into the kingdom of God – we enter in by means of our relationship with Him and because we have built our lives upon His words. Many will say to me in that day, Lord, Lord, have we not prophesied in thy name? and in thy name have cast out devils? and in thy name done many wonderful works? And then will I profess unto them, I never knew you: depart from me, ye that work iniquity. Therefore whosoever heareth these sayings of mine, and doeth them, I will liken him unto a wise man, which built his house upon a rock. (Matthew 7:22-24) I truly hope we connect with this unspoken reality – there will be many of us who will hear Him say, 'I never knew you, depart from me, you that work iniquity'.

These three dimensions that we have talked about also differ in terms of the nature of the source that provides and governs the light in which we walk and live. The outer court, which is a place outside the tabernacle or temple, only gets light from the natural world; the sun, moon and stars. So too, Christians who live in this outer court dimension, walk according to the flesh, and are thus influenced in life by that which is around them.

The seven-lamp candlestick provided light for the Holy place, and as we walk in the Christ dimension, it speaks of supernatural light, and of being led by the Spirit. The candlestick in fact is a mixture of spiritual things and natural things, whereas the outer court is pure natural light. The Word of God, represented in the tabernacle by the table of shew bread, also provides 'light'. *Thy word is a lamp unto my feet, and a light unto my path.* (Psalm 119:105) This speaks about being guided by the Word of God in terms of our decision-making.

The Most Holy place reflects the pure light of the Shekinah glory of God, which is a SUPERIOR-GOD-KIND-OF-LIGHT. *And there shall be no night there; and they need no candle, neither light of the sun; for the Lord God giveth them light: and they shall reign for ever and ever.* (Revelations 22:5) Here comes the scary untold part of the whole matter, the sun, moon and stars will be destroyed immediately after the tribulation, and the believers in the outer court will have no light to walk in, because they have never relied on the Word to be a lamp to their feet and a light to their path, nor did they rely on the Holy Spirit to lead and guide them. *Immediately after the tribulation of those days shall the sun be darkened, and the moon shall not give her light, and the stars shall fall from heaven, and the powers of the heavens shall be shaken.* (Matthew 24:29)

Now we may ask why God Almighty would want to destroy the sun, the moon and the stars. God will destroy them, because the sun, moon and stars are gods to many other religious groups among the nations. This is what Ezekiel saw - *And he brought me into the inner court of the LORD'S house, and, behold, at the door of the temple of the LORD, between the porch and the altar, were about five and twenty men, with their backs toward the temple of the LORD, and their faces* toward the east; and they worshipped the sun toward the east. (Ezekiel 8:16) **Indeed** He giveth us richly all things to enjoy. (1Timothy 6:17)

By worshiping the things that He created for their pleasure, God's created beings have turned much of His creation into His enemies. There is no other god that will be able to stand before God Almighty in the Day of His appearing. In fact God warns the Israelites not to worship the sun, moon and stars. And lest thou lift up thine eyes unto heaven, and when thou seest the sun, and the moon, and the stars, even all the host of heaven, shouldest be driven to worship them, and serve them, which the LORD thy God hath divided unto all nations under the whole heaven. (Deuteronomy 4:19)

The dimension we have lived or died in, will be the dimension in which we will live forever. I am referring to our relational dimension in God, whether it be the JESUS dimension (outer court), or the CHRIST dimension (Holy place), or the LORD dimension (Most Holy place). Ecclesiastes 11:3b further **explains this;** and if the tree fall toward the south, or toward the north, in the place where the tree fall, there it shall be. A tree speaks about human beings, therefore this verse actually says to us, the dimension in which a person dies, there he or she shall be. Isaiah 61: 3 calls us **'trees of righteousness'.**

This means a person who lived or died in the outer court dimension will live forever in darkness, because the very source that has given them light will be destroyed after the tribulation. But the children of the kingdom shall be cast out into outer darkness: there shall be weeping and gnashing of teeth. (Matthew 8:12) The Message Bible sheds greater light on this **scripture verse.** Then those who grew up 'in the faith' but had no faith will find themselves out in the cold, outsiders to grace and wondering what happened. **Remember!** Jesus asks this question in Matthew – will I find faith on the earth? The Bible also speaks about another group of believers who did not use their gifts and talents to advance the kingdom of God who will also be cast into the outer darkness. *And cast ye the unprofitable servant into outer darkness:* (Matthew 25:30)

Exodus 10: 22-23 provides us a picture of this reality; even though, there was thick darkness in all the land of Egypt for three days, all the children of Israel had light in their dwellings. In the very same way, the Christians who have lived or died in the 'Holy Place' and the 'Most Holy Place', will have light in their lives. But there shall be weeping and gnashing of teeth in the place called outer darkness, because this thick darkness is a felt darkness according to verse twenty-one. The darkness in Egypt was so thick that the Egyptians could not see one another, neither rose any from his place for three days while the darkness lasted. Not having a close relationship with the Lord is similar to this, even though we may be far more comfortable with the light of the sun, moon and stars, ie; being led by the flesh.

Any one of these three dimensions is a place of our own choice, because we all have equal access into God's presence by the blood of His Son. And our relationship with Him will get even better in our glorious future. We can now see that the message of getting saved to go to heaven, was simply an evangelical strategy, which made people afraid and led them to salvation, but on closer inspection, it is not a biblical truth.

Below is a table showing these three-dimensions in greater detail to better understand how God works with us. God is three-dimensional, we are three-dimensional, and His dealings with us are also three-dimensional.

1st DIMENSION	2nd DIMENSION	3rd DIMENSION
Outer court	Holy place	Most Holy place
Jesus	Christ	Lord
Passover feast	Pentecost feast	Tabernacle feast
His presence	His Anointing	His glory
Logos	Revelation/ Rhema	Oracles of God

Righteousness	Peace	Joy
Justify	Sanctify	Glorify
Egypt	Wilderness	Promise land
Body	Soul	Spirit
Responsibility	Accountability	Authority
The will of God - **good** Tabernacle of Moses 30 fold	The will of God - **acceptable** Temple of Solomon 60 fold	The will of God - **perfect** Jesus the true tabernacle 100 fold

The Church is now coming into the fullness of its third dimension, which is the picture in the third column.

THE FINAL DESTINATIONS OF SINNERS, BELIEVERS, AND TRUE DISCIPLES.

There are three places where the human race will spend eternity. The first destination is that belonging to the outer court believers, that is, those who did not pursue a personal relationship with the Lord; they will be cast into the outer darkness forever. This means their personal salvation has only saved them from burning in the eternal furnace of fire, yet, they will forever be separated from the LORD, because they have in fact lived their lives apart from Him even though they grew up in the faith. Revelation 11:1-2 is God's final judgment concerning outer court believers. *And there was given me a reed like unto a rod: and the angel stood, saying, Rise, and measure the temple of God, and the altar, and them that worship therein. But the court which is without the temple leave out, and measure it not; for it is given unto the Gentiles: and the holy city shall they tread under foot forty and two months.* The Father is seeking for those who can worship HIM in Spirit and in truth, nothing more and nothing less.

The outer court surrounded the Holy Place and the Most Holy Place, meaning that it bordered on the world outside. This speaks of believers, who are not completely separated from the world, and thereby do not have the power of God to positively influence and change it. Godly power, is found only in an abiding relationship with Christ, who is the power of God. Instead, outer courts Christians are being influenced by the world's way of doing things. This has brought worldly (Gentile) influences into the outer court, defiling it. I believe this is what God means when He says that the outer court dimension will be 'given to the Gentiles' and that He is not interested in measuring it.

The saints in the Holy Place and Most Holy place are the second group of people, and their destination is to inherit the kingdom of God; Then shall the King say unto them on his right hand, Come, ye blessed of my Father, inherit the kingdom prepared for you from the foundation of the world - (Matthew 25:34) Then shall the righteous shine forth as the sun in the kingdom of their Father. (Matthew 13:43) This group is made up of His true disciples who do not love their lives to the point of death; therefore they have come to know HIM as Jesus Christ the Lord.

The third group are those who have rejected Jesus Christ, therefore the Son of man shall send forth His angels, and they shall gather out of His kingdom all things that offend, and them which do iniquity; and shall cast them into a furnace of fire. (Matthew 13: 41,42) (This is the third place!) And the beast was taken, and with him the false prophet that wrought miracles before him, with which he deceived them that had received the mark of the beast, and them that worshiped his image. These both were cast alive into a lake of fire burning with brimstone (Revelations 19:20)

There is no middle ground, if a person does not accept the Lord as his personal Saviour, he indirectly accepts Satan as his Lord, and everything they do in the kingdom of darkness is accepted as worship by their god called Satan.

Chapter Eleven

FAITH FOR THE KINGDOM OF GOD

For the kingdom is the LORD'S: and he is the governor among the nations - (Psalm. 22:2)
As Christians we have certainly been taught well how to exercise our faith to benefit ourselves. We know how to use our faith to change things for our personal good; faith for our family's well-being; faith to meet our financial needs; faith for whatever we desire; faith to be healed; faith to see our children get saved; faith for when we are in trouble; faith for job promotions or salary increases; etc. Yet we hardly ever hear or know how to exercise our faith to see the kingdom of God established. We look at all the trouble in the world and we consciously or subconsciously think it is an impossible task to restore the terrible mess. I agree that it seems impossible, because with men this is impossible, but with God all things are possible; therefore, all things are possible to those who believe they are possible. *For with God nothing shall be impossible.* (Luke 1:37) Is anything too hard for God? I personally say, NO!

We must seriously develop the kind of faith in the kingdom of God that comes by hearing; that is, by hearing the Word of God regarding the message of His kingdom. We have been well taught to seek for all the promises of God which are yes and amen, and to get those promises from the pages of the Bible into our heads, dwelling on them until they get into our hearts and then confessing those promises until they manifest. We have learned well that the word in our hearts and in our mouths is the word of faith that produces effective results. How many of us have studied the word on the kingdom, and eagerly followed the very same process to develop faith; the kind of faith needed to see the kingdom of God established? Not many of us.

But now the time has come for God to lead us on to maturity and away from childish things. Let us not remain in ignorance and/or selfishness, as the LORD is drawing a line between those who seek His hands, and those who seek to hear His heart-beat and to understand His mind. The time and season has changed, because the LORD wants to accomplish His goal, which is the establishment of His kingdom. *And he said unto them, Go ye, and tell that fox, Behold, I cast out devils, and I do cures to day and to morrow, and the third day I shall be perfected. (Luke 13:32)* He is seeking for selfless believers who are willing to set aside their own personal agendas for the sake of His kingdom.

HERE IS A MIRROR QUESTION: On which side of the line are you standing? Are YOU one of those who stand on the opposite side to those who are willing to sacrifice everything for the sake of the kingdom? We need to seek out scripture verses concerning the kingdom of God and begin to establish these verses in our hearts, to develop strong faith for the kingdom's establishment on earth.

I am reminded of when I first heard a prosperity message; at that time of my life, I was financially disempowered - just plain broke really, and that message on prosperity was good news to me. I then got hold of a prosperity booklet and I studied that booklet thoroughly and intensively several times. I meditated on various prosperity scripture verses until my mind was totally and completely renewed on the subject called prosperity. I guess you know the blessed outcome. My financial life was totally changed and transformed – I moved from broke to prosperity. I am now well able to prove to others that the will of God concerning our financial life is **good, acceptable and perfect.**

In the same way I began to study the reality of the kingdom of God and it changed my outlook on life. Instead of being motivated to look forward to getting to heaven, thus escaping the earth, I am now more than ever determined to grow up to possess the kingdom of God, and to drive out the darkness in the world with the light of His Word by preaching the good news of the kingdom.

We must develop faith for the kingdom to avoid being gullible to teachings based on the bad news in the world. Let us not, having enjoyed the blessings and prosperity of the LORD, now look to escape all the trouble in the world. We will certainly seek this sort of escape if we do not develop our capacity to handle troubling situations in the world. This is exactly what the Israelites did – they were happy when things were going well for them, but the very moment they were tested, they wanted to escape their circumstances by going back to Egypt. Saints of God, that is an ugly, horrible spirit that the Body of Christ has to get rid of. We are going nowhere. We are here to stay, until we are a blessing to the LORD our God, who has been a tremendous and an amazing blessing to us.

In teaching and sharing prophetically concerning these end-times, let us also be aware that the Book of Revelation is a revelation of Jesus Christ. *The Revelation of Jesus Christ, which God gave unto him, to show unto his servants things which must shortly come to pass; and he sent and signified it by his angel unto his servant John: Who bare record of the word of God, and of the testimony of Jesus Christ, and of all things that he saw. (Revelation 1:1-2)*

The Book of Revelation is **not** a revelation of the anti-Christ, neither is it a revelation of the beast or the false prophet. Yet we seem to hear very little being shared about Jesus Christ and the victory that He has accomplished for us. Unfortunately many end-time teachers major on all the bad news in the world, plus the revelation of the anti-Christ, the beast and the false prophet, thus totally overshadowing the revelation of Jesus Christ. This invokes fear in the hearts of believers, and so the rapture seems to be a sensible thing to them. Let us pray for the Spirit of revelation and wisdom to give us a greater revelation of Jesus Christ and the VICTORY He has accomplished for us. Our responsibility is to take that spiritual victory by faith and convert it into an objective reality in our personal lives and in the world.

Let's face this reality: when confronted with negativity we tend to make it our focus and concern. This is because negativity impresses itself forcefully on us, and the positive side of the matter is not immediately apparent. Therefore many of us tend to give more attention to negativity instead of seeking out the positive of the matter, keeping in mind that any matter can be likened to a coin with a picture on both sides.   Let me explain this further by a biblical example from Daniel 7:17; These great beasts, which are four, are four kings, which shall arise out of the earth. We tend to give more attention to this verse and far less attention to the very next verse, which says, But the saints of the most High shall take the kingdom, and possess the kingdom for ever, even for ever and ever. BUT... 'But' means 'on the contrary' or 'rather than'. Contrary means opposite in nature or opposite in direction or position. Instead of seeking to get a clearer revelation of verse eighteen, we tap into the knowledge of these great beasts which shall arise out of the earth, and we end up preaching hundreds of series and writing many books on verse seventeen, saying nothing about verse eighteen. This is exactly what we did with the book of Revelation. No wonder the LORD closed the book of Revelation with these words. For I testify unto every man that heareth the words of the prophecy of this book, If any man shall add unto these things, God shall add unto him the plagues that are written in this book: (Revelations 22:18) And if any man shall take away from the words of the book of this prophecy, God shall take away his part out of the book of life, and out of the holy city, and from the things which are written in this book. (Revelations 22:19)

Is it really true that the GREAT TRIBULATION will make all victories and overcoming promises of no effect? Is the great tribulation so great that the Word of God will not work for us during these troubling times? Is there any secret interpretation that says the spoken word of God will not work for the saints of God during the great tribulation? Well, Jesus did not say so, but this is what He did say: For verily I say unto you, Till heaven and earth pass, one jot or one tittle shall in no wise pass from the law, till all be fulfilled. (Matthew 5:18)

God's Law is more real and more lasting than the stars in the sky and the ground at our feet. Long after stars burn out and earth wears out, God's Law will be alive and working. Let us allow these questions to stimulate our thinking and graciously assist us to realize that the rapture theory is a man-made doctrine. Even the various viewpoints on these rapture theories confirm the nature of man-made doctrines. There is no way that these different groups would ever come into the unity of the faith. Let us now have a close look at all the different viewpoints on the rapture, second coming, and Millennium viewpoints and ask ourselves why God would cause so much confusion.

There is a:

    Premillennial Pretribulational view.

    Premillennial Posttribulational view.

    Premillennial Midtribulational view.

    Premillenial Pretribulational Partial Rapture view.

    Premillennial Prewrath Rapture view.

    Evangelical Postmillennial view.

    St. Augustine's Amillennial view.

    A second Amillennial view.

My sincere intention is to show just how many different view-points there are concerning the rapture theory. I have no interest in explaining these different view points, as they do nothing but cause much disunity in the Body of Christ. The purpose of the five-fold ministry is not to separate the Body of Christ, but to bring all saints into the unity of the faith. We are here on earth to complete each other not to compete with each other's different viewpoints. I therefore beseech all of us by the mercies of God not to be drawn into these kinds of disunity debates and discussions. *But avoid foolish questions, and genealogies, and contentions, and strivings about the law; for they are unprofitable and vain. (Titus 3:9)* Competition always leads to self exaltation, especially when it comes to viewpoints contrary to the spoken word of God.

Till heaven and earth pass, one jot or tittle shall in no wise pass from the law, till all the overcoming verses that have been given to us, are fulfilled. We are therefore encouraged to develop strong faith to withstand any hardship. *Thou therefore endure hardness, as a good soldier of Jesus Christ. (2 Timothy 2:3)* Let us rather prepare ourselves for the great tribulation, instead of bargaining on a rapture; please cancel your flight ticket to heaven and prepare yourself to establish the kingdom of God. We are all needed on the earth. We will meet Him in the air to make Him King on earth, not to go back to heaven with Him. 1 Thessalonians 4: 17 does not say we will meet Him in the air and so shall we ever be with the Lord in heaven. Meeting Him in the air is a courtesy, just like you would go to meet your guest by the gate or door when they come to visit you.

In Matthew 4 Jesus set a clear example to us when He was tempted by the devil, He spoke the Word saying, 'it is written...' and the devil departed from Him; *Then the devil leaveth him, and, behold, angels came and ministered unto him. (Matthew 4:11)* Here Jesus shows us by example, what Adam and Eve should have done when they were tempted by the devil. All these following overcoming verses are yes and amen. *For all the promises of God in him are yea, and in him Amen, unto the glory of God by us. (2 Corinthians 1:20)*

SCRIPTURE VERSES ON OVERCOMING DURING THE GREAT TRIBULATION:

Romans 8:35-39 - Who shall separate us from the love of Christ? Shall tribulation, or distress, or persecution, or famine, or nakedness, or peril, or sword? As it is written, For thy sake we are killed all the day long; we are accounted as sheep for the slaughter. Nay, in all these things we are more than conquerors through him that loved us. For I am persuaded, that neither death, nor life, nor angels, nor principalities, nor powers, nor things present, nor things to come, Nor height, nor depth, nor any other creature, shall be able to separate us from the love of God, which is in Christ Jesus our Lord.

Luke 10:18-19 - And he said unto them, I beheld Satan as lightning fall from heaven. Behold, I give unto you power to tread on serpents and scorpions, and over all the power of the enemy: and nothing shall by any means hurt you.

1John 5:4 - For whatsoever is born of God overcometh the world: and this is the victory that overcometh the world, even our faith.

1John 5:5 - Who is he that overcometh the world, but he that believeth that Jesus is the Son of God? John 16:33 - These things I have spoken unto you, that in me ye might have peace. In the world ye shall have tribulation: but be of good cheer; I have overcome the world.

Revelation 12:11 - And they overcame him by the blood of the Lamb, and by the word of their testimony; and they loved not their lives unto the death.

Isaiah 54:17 - No weapon which is formed against thee shall prosper; and every tongue that shall rise against thee in judgment thou shalt condemn. This is the heritage of the servants of the LORD, and their righteousness is of me, saith the LORD.

Deuteronomy 20:3 - And shall say unto them, Hear, O Israel (O Church), ye approach this day unto battle against your enemies: let not your hearts faint, fear not, and do not tremble, neither be ye terrified because of them; For the LORD your God is he that goeth with you, to fight for you against your enemies, to save you.

Psalm 9:9-10 - The LORD also will be a refuge for the oppressed, a refuge in times of trouble. And they that know thy name will put their trust in thee: for thou, LORD, hast not forsaken them that seek thee.

1 John 4:4 - Ye are of God, little children, and have overcome them: because greater is he that is in you, than he that is in the world.

1 John 5:4 For whatsoever is born of God overcometh the world: and this is the victory that overcometh the world, even our faith.

We are far more than conquerors with all these scripture verses in our hearts and mouths. These verses have always worked very well; therefore, they will also work during the days of the great tribulation. If we believe more in the power of the great tribulation than in the Word, we may as well tear these scripture verses out of the Bible to please our fearful selves. Concerning the great tribulation, we need the heart and mind of Shadrach, Meshach, and Abednego, who said to the king,

O Nebuchadnezzar, we are not careful to answer thee in this matter. If it be so, our God whom we serve is able to deliver us from the burning fiery furnace, and he will deliver us out of thine hand, O king. But if not, be it known unto thee, O king, that we will not serve thy gods, nor worship the golden image which thou hast set up. (Daniel 3:16b-18)

ISRAEL IS NATURAL AND THE CHURCH IS SPIRITUAL.

The Israelites in the Old Testament experienced everything in the natural that we experience spiritually. They had a real experience of the real Egypt, of the real wilderness and the real Canaan (their promised land). They had to face real enemies and real hot blood was shed when they engaged those enemies. These natural experiences are very helpful for us to learn from, because today we also have an 'Egypt', a 'wilderness', a 'promised land' and an enemy to fight. These are a Christian's unseen realities. Our wrestle is not against real flesh and blood, rather we are dealing with unseen enemies which can be paralleled in the history of the Israelites. For though we walk in the flesh, we do not war after the flesh. (2 Corinthians 10:3) We can therefore greatly benefit by looking into Israel's historical experiences to understand our present spiritual realities - Howbeit that was not first which is spiritual, but that which is natural; and afterward that which is spiritual. (1 Corinthians 15:46)

In this instance we definitely need to look at all the kingdom dynamics of the Israelites in their journey from Egypt through the wilderness into their promised land, and look at how God took them through many different kinds of experiences to fulfill the spoken word He gave them in Exodus 19:6a And ye shall be unto me a kingdom of priests, and a holy nation. In this way we can develop kingdom faith because if God could do it for them, He will also do it for us. As a matter of fact we have received the same promise, which is recorded in the Book of 1 Peter 2:9; But ye are a chosen generation, a royal priesthood, an holy nation, a peculiar people; that ye should show forth the praises of him who hath called you out of darkness into marvelous light. The development of corporate leadership is just one of the principles beautifully illustrated by Israel's history. God first chose one man (Moses), to lead an entire nation; then God connected this man to his father-in-law, Jethro. Jethro adviced Moses to adopt a totally new leadership idea based on a team concept. This eventually enabled the people of Israel to progress from the team concept into corporate leadership, as God's ultimate aim for Israel was to have a priestly kingdom. God's desire has not changed! It is still for a kingdom of priests, who can rule and reign the earth corporately.

On the other hand, the world's way of ruling is to exercise lordship over people for personal gain. Jesus puts it like this in Luke 22: 25-26 *And he said unto them, The kings of the Gentiles exercise lordship over them; and they that exercise authority upon them are called benefactors. But ye shall not be so: but he that is greatest among you, let him be as the younger; and he that is chief, as he that doth serve.* The only reason God appointed judges over the people was because of their inability to rule themselves from within; therefore there was a need for external government. Scripture shows that the role of judges became obsolete as it was only ever a temporary arrangement.

God's way of ruling is for leaders to serve His people with everything He gave them. This kind of leadership style produces greatness, which makes us a perculiar special people, above all people. Leaders need to train their people servitude by being an example of servant-hood. The success of a leader should be a reflection of the success of the people they lead. Even the most successful marriages are the result of couples who have found their greatest enjoyment in serving each other selflessly. The root cause of most divorce is selfishness.

This three-dimensional leadership development can also be seen in the Church. There has been a season in the Church of one man taking the lead and the rest of the people following. This season is long over and now there is no more room in the Body of Christ for lone-rangers. Being a lone-ranger nowadays is a very dangerous thing. Thank God Almighty for the restoration of the five-fold ministry and for bringing the Church into a team-based leadership concept, and for establishing networks across the Body of Christ. This has indeed maximized our effectiveness in the Body of Christ. Yet, team-based leadership is not God's ultimate desire for the Church. He longs for the Corporate Body to function in the same way the team-based leadership and networks are functioning. We should keep in mind that the five-fold ministries will cease to exist once they have fulfilled their purpose, which is to bring the Church into a corporate leadership dimension and thereby actively create a kingdom of priests – a kingdom people who can rule the earth corporately as kings and priests. Thus, once this goal is accomplished the five-fold ministry will become obsolete, just like the judges, priests, prophets and the kings in the Old Testament.

There will not be a need for leaders to be appointed over God's people once we all have come to the unity of the faith, and of the knowledge of the Son of God, unto a perfect man, unto the measure of the stature of the fullness of Christ. God gave leadership responsibility to both Adam and Eve at the start – we are designed to rule together. *And they shall not teach every man his neighbor, and every man his brother, saying, Know the Lord: for all shall know me, from the least to the greatest.* (Hebrews 8:11) This in a nutshell means people will become less dependent on leaders, so that they can independently deal with their own problems and difficulties or minister to one another to resolve personal problems and matters.

A practical example is being under the leadership of our parents until we mature and start our own family. We do not really need the leadership of our parents once we mature and have our own family. It is impossible to become interdependent if we are not independent. Interdependence is the gate-way to corporate leadership. Understanding this sequence of ongoing growth should make us all passionate about the Church, stopping any negative talk about HER, building HER up, and getting seriously involved in kingdom business until this GREAT GIANT (The Church) arises in the fullness of God's power and glory. I have nothing else to live for, because anything else has no eternal and lasting value, only the eternal kingdom of God does. By putting the kingdom first, we can have what others seek for. *But seek ye first the kingdom of God, and his righteousness; and all these things shall be added unto you* (Matthew 6:33)

ISRAEL'S DEVELOPMENT PROCESS HAS EVENTUALLY PRODUCED AN ESTABLISHED KINGDOM IN ISRAEL.

Let me reconnect you again to God's purpose for mankind. God wanted to have a kingdom of priests ruling and reigning in the earth as kings and priests unto God their ultimate KING. It was not God's intention to have an earthly king or leader to rule over His people. This is very evident when the Israelites wanted to have a king just like all the other nations. They had rejected God their KING, because they did not want Him to reign over them. They came to *Samuel And said unto him, Behold, thou art old, and thy sons walk not in thy ways: now make us a king to judge us like all the nations. But the thing displeased Samuel, when they said, Give us a king to judge us. And Samuel prayed unto the LORD. And the LORD said unto Samuel, Hearken unto the voice of the people in all that they say unto thee: for they have not rejected thee, but they have rejected me, that I should not reign over them.* (1 Samuel 8:5-8) Actually God allowed this to happen, because Israel was a type or shadow of what was to come.

This shadow paints a very clear picture for us to see the progressive growth process, which is an unseen process in us. A picture says more than a thousand words. God foretold all the problems they would experience by wanting a mere man to be their king, when God Himself was the only perfect king. King Saul was a selfish king who really did not have a heart after God. It never crossed his mind to return the ark back to Israel during his reign, and ultimately his kingdom could not be established, because he disobeyed the LORD his God. This kind of leadership was and still is very evident in the Body of Christ – leaders who have an arrogant, self-serving, and one-man-show kind of attitude, which is a Saul-spirit. The LORD is about to bring judgment on this kind of leadership style, just like He has judged Saul. The LORD judged Saul long after He had raised up David and anointed him king over Israel.

Today there is no doubt there are many David's in the Body of Christ, who have been raised up and anointed by God for a time such as this. Their leadership style is evident by them dwelling among the people of God, just like Jesus, who walked, slept, ate and drunk with His disciples. There is no way that Saul would have danced naked in front of the people, because the Saul-spirit tends to separate itself from the people. The David's in the Body are hidden and will soon arise as God begins to judge the Saul type of leadership in the Body of Christ.

These are hard sayings that will soon become a hard painful reality in the Body of Christ. David, unlike Saul had no desire to establish his own kingdom. This Saul-spirit can be seen in leaders who are overly-ambitious at the expense of the people, building their own ministries with no sincere regard for the kingdom of God. God chose David above Saul, because he had a sincere heart after God. The Saul kind of leadership is based on deeply embedded insecurities, and the David kind of inspirational leader is based on finding security in God. People who sincerely long to see the kingdom of God established at the expense of what is dear to them have a heart after God, because God's longing is also to see His kingdom established in all the earth.

Something very interesting to notice is that David's kingly ministry was very effective, even while Saul was still king. David was not waiting passively day-dreaming about sitting upon the throne, he was busy doing the will of God. This can also be said concerning the Davids of our day and time; they are actively busy doing the will of God while they may still be unknown to the many. They will only come to the forefront when God has judged the present-day Sauls. This can also be seen by the ministry of John and Jesus. Jesus was in the background, while Johns ministry was still in the forefront. Jesus' ministry came to the forefront only when John was beheaded. The following verse is a sign and an indication of where the Church finds itself right now. Read these words that Nathan said to David according to the vision he had. *And thine house and thy kingdom shall be established forever before thee: thy throne shall be established forever.* (2 Samuel 7:16) Now is the time to develop faith for the kingdom, because the kingdom of God will be established in our day and time as the David generation begins to arise. The energetic deep worship and explosive praise that God is releasing in the Church are signs that the David generation is arising in the power of His might. God Almighty is actively involved in destroying all the enemies who are opposing His kingdom rule, which is exactly what God did through the leadership of King David. God is destroying His enemies in every nation as we boldly proclaim the message of the good news of the kingdom of God as a witness to all nations. We are the generation that will establish the kingdom of God upon the earth for the peace of God to finally rule and reign in the hearts and minds of all the people upon the earth.

It is the Solomon generation that will usher in the peace of God upon the earth. *Then sat Solomon upon the throne of David his father; and his kingdom was established greatly.* (1 Kings 2:12) The David generation will destroy all the enemies of God to pave the way for our next generation to live in total peace. We will miss the purposes of God if we wrongly perceive that heaven is the place where we will enjoy peace and rest from our enemies. The Old Testament is a picture of the real thing we have been hoping and praying for. Behold, a son shall be born to thee, who shall be a man of rest; and I will give him rest from all his enemies round about: for his name shall be Solomon, and I will give peace and quietness unto Israel in his days. (1 Corinthians 22:9) This verse can be rewritten for us today as; "Behold, a new generation shall be born to thee, who shall be a generation of rest; and I will give them rest from all their enemies (principalities, powers, rulers and wicked spirits) round about: for their name shall be the Solomon Generation, and I will give peace and quietness unto My Church in Her days."

Can you see why I am saying we should gradually develop faith for the establishment of God's kingdom on earth? With our human understanding it may be too hard to believe this kind of life is possible upon the earth; therefore, we need to meditate on scriptures regarding the kingdom of God in order to establish faith for it. Let's have a look at the outcome of Solomon's kingdom and step back and ask ourselves whether the Israelites could have ever imagined, or have hoped and had faith for such a kingdom after 430 years of oppression in Egypt. ......and Solomon reigned <u>over all kingdoms</u> from the river unto the land of the Philistines, and unto the border of Egypt: they brought presents, and served Solomon all the days of his life. (1 Kings 4:21) Do you honestly think that the Israelites would have believed if Moses had told them that there would come a day in their lives that they would reign over all kingdoms?

I will now show you the vision that Apostle John saw regarding us, and see how similar it looks to Solomon's reign. And the seventh angel sounded; and there were great voices in heaven, saying, The kingdoms of this (modern) world are become the kingdoms of our Lord, and of his Christ (His Church); and he shall reign forever and ever. (Revelations 11:15) If God did it for the Israelites, how much more will He do it for us, because the New Covenant holds better promises than the Old Covenant. But now hath he obtained a more excellent ministry, by how much also he is the mediator of a better covenant, which was established upon better promises. For if that first covenant had been faultless, then should no place have been sought for the second. (Hebrews 8:6-7) Let me also add the need for a second covenant: the shadow of the real thing passed away, but the new will be forever.

God has set up His kingdom and it shall never be destroyed by the kingdom of darkness, and the kingdom shall be left to none other than us. And in the days of these kings shall the God of heaven set up a kingdom, which shall never be destroyed: and the kingdom shall not be left to other people, but it shall break in pieces and consume all these kingdoms, and it shall stand forever. (Daniel 2:44) The kingdom of God is an everlasting kingdom with no other rule interrupting it. Therefore, it no longer makes sense for us to be raptured and leave the earth completely in the hands and rulership of the devil and his foes, and still claim the kingdom of God to be an everlasting kingdom. This is unacceptable; we will not leave the earth in the hands of the devil's evil control for him to do whatever he wants. He is free to do what He wants to do in the pit of hell prepared for him and his foes. We cannot preach rapture plus kingdom, as they are opposing concepts. The one says, let's fly away O glory and the other says, 'let's take over.' I hear the voice of Joshua saying, **"we are ready to go up and to possess the land"**. God's heart longs to hear such a voice coming from all His people, in these last days.

Chapter Twelve

THE MAKING OF KINGS

And hath made us kings and priests unto God and his Father; to him be glory and dominion for ever and ever. Amen. (Revelation 1:6)

Everyone is doing what is right in their own eyes in every nation, due to the fact that there are no kings on the earth, even though we have been made kings. We have not yet taken Revelation 1: 6 as a serious matter. We are focusing too much on being Christians, which was a name that the pagans gave the Christians in Antioch. *And the disciples were called Christians first in Antioch (Act 11:26.)* Saints we are suppose to be kings on the earth – let us go beyond being mere Christians. We are citizens of the Kingdom of God and members of the household of God. The Church is our house and the kingdom of God is our inheritance.

Judges 17:6 In those days there was no king in Israel, but every man did that which was right in his own eyes. The presence of a King brings a sense of restrain and refrains in a nation. The people did not do what was right in their own eyes when there was a king in Israel, which represent the Church in our day and time. Much changes will begin to happen in every nation when the message of the good news of the Kingdon of God is preached in every nation and the saints of God begin to awaken to their call as Kings.

THE LORD IS IN THE BUSINESS OF RAISING UP KINGS IN EVERY NATION.

The LORD led the Israelites on a journey through the wilderness to restore them from everything that had happened to them in Egypt. This time of slavery diminished their true identity and God-nature by a relentless chain of severe life experiences under the rulership of a Pharaoh who, today, can represent a type of the devil in our lives. *And they* (Egyptians) *made their* (Israelites) *lives bitter with hard service, in mortar and in brick, and in all manners of service in the field, all their service, wherein they made them serve with rigor.* (Exodus 1:14) As a result, the LORD shared with them this promise to give them a sense of hope. *I will accept you as My people, and I will be your God. Then you will know that I was the one who rescued you from the Egyptians.* (Exodus 6:7)

The journey the Israelites traveled from Egypt into their promised land was their development process to become the special people God intended them to be, a people above all people that are upon the face of the earth. Whatever they went through between Egypt and the promised land was an intense process that revealed a rebellious nature, a rebellion born of their years of slavery.

Unbearable situations and circumstances have two opposing results depending on our personal response; either they will eventually bring out the very best in us, or we will gradually become deformed in character. The outcome depends on how we choose to relate to the worst part of ourselves exposed by our oppressive 'trials'. Shame has a way of opening up our hearts to invite change, yet some people adapt to their shameful state and continue to live in it. The worse part of us, exposed by layers of negative life experiences, hides the true person created in the image and likeness of God.

The best leaders in the world are those who have worked their way out of terribly unbearable life circumstances. The people who travel the path of least resistance become the least in the world, but those who travel the path of great opposition, become the greatest in the world. Just as resistance training at the gym produces muscles, so too inner resistance training produces a person of distinctive quality, substance and capacity.

Ex- president Nelson Mandela of South Africa is a classic example of a leader who has been in the wilderness for many years, but his outcome was marvelous. Sometimes it takes a painful experience to make us change our ways. (Proverbs 20:30) There are not many leaders who have the patience and wisdom to endure the distress and bad behaviour of their people until the 'best' in them surfaces.

Jesus is the finest example of a leader who endured His walk with His twelve disciples for three long years until they became profitable for kingdom purposes. None of us came out of our personal Egypt as vessels of honour prepared for every good work for the Master. Every negative undealt hurt, pain, disappointment, rejection, offense, bitterness, unforgiveness, sense of worthlessness, etc has the destructive power and the driving force to make all of us vessels of dishonour; therefore, we all need a 'wilderness' experience to purge us. If a man therefore purge himself from these (above mentioned), he shall be a vessel unto honour, sanctified, and meet for the master's use, and prepared unto every good work. (2 Timothy 2:21)

The Israelites went through their wilderness for forty years, even though there was a shorter route to the Promised land. The way they behaved themselves on their journey revealed what was in them; therefore, the LORD did not lead them via the shorter route, because He wanted to cleanse Eygpt's ways and the results of Egypt's oppression from their lives.

The sinful world we have been translated from or brought out of by the blood of Jesus is our Egypt. Who hath delivered us from the power of darkness (Egypt), and hath translated us into the kingdom of his dear Son. (Colossians 1:13) This means we too have to be cleansed from all the things we have learned in Egypt which are contrary to God's way of doing things. We too must be cleansed from the results of negative experiences in Egypt. The LORD gave to us, His New Testament Church, exactly the same word He gave to the Israelites. *But ye are a chosen generation, a royal priesthood, a holy nation, a peculiar people (a kingdom people); that ye should show forth the praises of him who hath called you out of darkness into his marvellous light. (1 Peter 2:9)*

The LORD has the same determination to see this word fulfilled in our lives, just as He did with the Israelites. He has made us to subdue the earth and to have dominion over all the works of His hands. Therefore, we too are subject to a necessary process of becoming a royal priesthood, a holy nation, a peculiar people, that we should shew forth the praises of Him who has called us out of the kingdom of darkness into the Kingdom of His dear Son Jesus Christ.

We are already a royal priesthood, a holy nation, a peculiar people in a subjective sense of the word, but the current reality is, we are not yet there. As we go through this process of becoming, we have to maintain the belief that we are already a royal priesthood, a holy nation, a peculiar people in a subjective sense, and that the purpose of the process is to upgrade our soul dimension to manifest this reality. It is not enough to know who we are in Christ Jesus; we need to positively experience and see this REALITY in our day-to-day lives.

I have heard it said, the Church does not have to go through a wilderness experience, because the Israelites could have completed their journey in only a few days, if only they had not complained and murmured. Here is a question for reflection – can we really expect anything better than complaints from a person who is negative due to the many negative experiences he or she has had? The heart of man can be likened to a bank account – every deposit we make builds up the account. In the same way, whatever we experience in life, whether good or bad, creates deposits filling up our emotional bank account.

The real you will always come to the fore under tremendous pressure. Pressure makes a withdrawal from what we have in our emotional account. Who we are, is not really who we are when everything is normal in our life – who we really are can only be discovered under pressure. A lemon squirts out lemon juice when it gets squeezed. In the same way, when pressure squeezes us we tend to bring forth who we really are deep within. 2 Chronicles 32:31b confirms this: *God left him, to try him, that he might know all that was in his heart.*

The Father knows what is in our hearts; therefore He sets us up, that we too might see more clearly that which we carry deep within. Having said all that, the time is now upon us when God is beginning to call His Church out of the wilderness. In the meantime Christians are despised by the unrighteous, because who we really are is not yet understood by them. Neither do they understand that we have all this time been a work in progress.

It is of the highest importance for us to make a connection with the Israelites and their experiences, as examples for our own lives as Christians. *For whatsoever things were written before were written for our learning, that we through patience and comfort of the Scriptures might have hope. (Romans 15:4)* The Israelites stand before us as a shadow or type of the real thing; we, on the other hand, are enormously privileged to be actually living the REAL thing. Therefore it is important for us to have some sort of understanding of the shadows and types set before us in the Old Testament, to be able to live the REAL thing in a way that is pleasing to God. May the LORD grant us grace, so that we might not become what Paul wrote about in 2Timothy 3:7 *Ever learning, and never able to come to the knowledge of the truth.* Therefore, we should buy the truth and sell it not – our FREEDOM is dependent on our knowledge of the TRUTH. *Buy the truth, and sell it no; also wisdom, and instruction, and understanding (Proverbs 23:23)*

The Israelites' process was a natural experience; they were in a real land called Egypt - a real wilderness, and they faced real enemies, which were flesh and blood and ultimately, they also experienced a real promised land that was filled with great abundance. We are subject to a similar process, but our experience is a spiritual one – we came out of Egypt, but in a spiritual sense; we too are having spiritual wilderness experiences, which are intensively emotional at times; we too face unseen enemies; *For, we wrestle not against flesh and blood, but against principalities, against powers, against the rulers of the darkness of this world, against spiritual wickedness in high places (Ephesians 6:12),* and ultimately we will also enter our promised land, which is a land of more than enough, and a place of ruling and reigning with Christ in the NOW, as well as in the Age to come.

Our promised land is our spiritual inheritance, which is all the nations of the earth and the uttermost parts of the earth, which altogether makes up the vastness of the kingdom of God; *Ask of me, and I will give thee the nations for thine inheritance, And the uttermost parts of the earth for thy possession.* (Psalm 2:8) *Hearken, my beloved brethren, Hath not God chosen the poor of this world rich in faith, and heirs of the kingdom which he hath promised to them that love him? (James 2:5)*

This spiritual journey can also be defined as a journey to wholeness, which requires great patience. We develop this kind of patience in the midst of our trials and tribulations, and it works patience in us that we may be perfect and complete, wanting nothing. *But let patience have her perfect work, that ye may be perfect and entire, wanting nothing. (James 1:4)* This journey is also known as our walk with God – in this walk we make great discoveries about who we are and who He is. We get to know God in the midst of our trouble as we experience His hand of protection, His healing power, His deliverance, His peace that surpasses our human understanding, His love when we feel rejected and His provision when there seems to be no way. Every new discovery of who God is automatically brings about a recovery of who we are meant to be.

Here is something very crucial to understand in order for us to make sense of this seemingly never-ending journey: everything the Bible says about us is a finished work in our spirit-being, but not in our soul-realm experience. Our spirit bears witness with Christ's finished work in us, but we feel confused and full of doubt within our soul. That's why the renewing of our mind is such an important aspect of our Christian life. *And be not conformed to this world: but be ye transformed by the renewing of your mind, that ye may prove what is that good, and acceptable and perfect, will of God (Romans 12:2)* The bad experiences that we have had in life, and still carry in our soul make it very hard to believe that the work is indeed finished; therefore, we must be careful that we do not fall into unbelief, because our unbelief slows down the manifestation of the finished work that needs to be worked out in our soul. *Now the just shall live by faith: but if any man draw back, my soul shall have no pleasure in him. (Hebrews 10:38)*

It is our soul that causes us to experience the kind of life we enjoy or fail to enjoy. Keeping in mind that; *...the LORD God formed man of the dust of the ground, and breathed into his nostrils the breath of life; and man became a living soul. (Genesis 2:7)* We have to keep our faith, believing that whatever we go through is to work out the finished work of Christ in our soul-dimension, and that this will eventually flow out into our natural lives as a real life experience. *In your patience possess ye your souls. (Luke 21:19)* The BBE version puts it like this: *By going through all these things, you will keep your lives.* Unbelief affects our walk with God, because anything we do in doubt is sin. Moreover, sin in itself has a manner of working against us and slows down our ongoing growth process. It is truly by grace through faith that we can in fact manage to live our lives in these two different kinds of realities.

HOW TO LIVE WITH TWO OPPOSING REALITIES

We must consider the spiritual REALITY a finished reality, and the other a temporary circumstantial reality, which is subject to change as we learn to focus our attention on our spiritual REALITY. This is all very easy to say on paper, because the temporary reality seems to be more real as we can see it, feel it, touch it, at times smell it and even taste it. No wonder the Apostle Paul admonishes us to walk by faith and not by sight (or according to our physical senses). *For we walk by faith, not by sight (2 Corinthians 5:7)* Believe me, our sight or temporary reality seems to dominate most of us, because it requires much time alone with God in prayer and reading, studying and meditating on the spoken word to get our faith REALITY at the same level as our sight reality. When this does happen, we begin to see how our sight reality becomes non-existent and our unseen REALITY becomes our day-to-day reality. Here is a classic example of what I am talking about: God has already provided all our needs and wants according to His riches in glory by Christ Jesus, but our sight reality says we are in want, or we are in need.

The reality we focus on and talk about the most is the reality we will eventually experience as our final reality. Our lesser reality is a seen reality and our greater reality is an unseen reality. Our spiritual goal on this journey is to make the unseen reality our seen reality whenever we are confronted with these two realities; this we might call a dilemma. Here is another example: when God looks at us through the flowing blood of His Son, He sees us perfect, complete and holy, but we on the other hand experience imperfection, incompleteness and un-holiness in our soul and in our day-to-day life experiences. Again, the final reality in this regard will depend on which reality we focus on the most and speak the most about. Jesus clearly said to us, we will have whatever we say. *For verily I say unto you, That whosoever shall say unto this mountain, Be* thou removed, and be thou cast into the sea; and shall not doubt in his heart, but shall believe that those things which he saith shall come to pass; he shall have whatsoever he saith. (Mark 11:23)

It would do us well to join our voices with the father of the dumb boy in Mark 9:24 who cried out, and said with tears, Lord, I believe: help thou mine unbelief that there is a greater REALITY that has the divine power and energy of God to overrule my lesser reality. According as his divine power hath given unto us all things that pertain unto life and godliness, through the knowledge of him that hath called us to glory and virtue (2 Peter 1:3) This is indeed the key to unlocking great success on this long and at times, painful journey. 2 Corinthians 4:18 summarizes this so beautifully. While we look not at the (scary) things which are seen, but at the things which are not seen: for the things which are seen are temporal; but the things which are not seen are eternal. Anything of eternal value will always rule over that which is temporary, because anything which is temporary is subject to change, but eternal things never change. We will also experience the reality of much pain and affliction on this journey, but the greater REALITY is that these things presently work for us, even though we strongly assume, see and feel that the affliction is working against us. For our light affliction, which is but for a moment, worketh for us a far more exceeding and eternal weight of glory. (2 Corinthians 4:17)

None of us is born with the essential power to FOCUS effectively, even though some of us are much stronger than others. Truthfully we tend to focus better on things that work against us instead of focusing on a thought or bible verse or our knowledge of what the goodness of God can work for us. The required power to focus on something positive or on a bible promise is a vital skill to develop in order for us to make progress on our spiritual journey. Whatever we focus on we empower, and whatever we empower will either work against us or for us. It is critical to develop our ability to focus on what God says about any situation or circumstance we face, instead of focusing on the report of the devil (eg. condemnation and lies), or the report of negative or critical people.

Learn to focus more effectively on your greater realities rather than your lesser realities. Whatever this world gives to us is a lesser reality, and whatever the BIBLE says to us is our greater reality. The Israelites made the biggest mistake of their lives to focus mostly on what went wrong (their lesser reality); they believed the story of the devil and doubted the report of the LORD.

An example in the New Testament is that of Peter walking on water in Matthew 14. Jesus' word to Peter to walk on the water was Peter's greater reality, and the law of nature telling him he couldn't, was his lesser reality. Peter could walk on water because his focus was directed on Jesus and the word 'come', and not on the law of nature which shouted 'you can't!' Then, when all was going miraculously well, his focus began to change. His eyes shifted from Jesus and looked upon the stormy sea, and *when he saw the wind boisterous, he was afraid; and beginning to sink, he cried, saying, Lord, save me.* (Matthew 14:30) As Christians we are supposed to live supernatural lives, focusing on our greater reality; we will most definitely sink if we focus on our lesser reality. This is a powerful lesson for kingdom rulers – we can all eventually rule over every situation and circumstance if we develop the essential ability to focus effectively on our greater reality, looking to Jesus, the author and finisher of our faith.

OUR WILDERNESS HAS THE POTENTIAL TO BE A LIFE CHANGING WORKSHOP EXPERIENCE

DEPENDING ON HOW WE REACT TO WHAT HAPPENS TO US.

We have no control over what happens to us, but we do have control over how we react or respond to what happens within us. How we react or respond determines our outcome in life. We see in scripture that Jesus Himself was led by the Spirit into the wilderness for forty days to be tempted by the devil *And he was there in the wilderness forty days, tempted of Satan; and was with the wild beasts; and the angels ministered unto him* (Mark 1:13) so that He could be the first among many brothers. This makes Jesus a leader worth following, because the best way to lead is to lead by example.

Have you ever noticed a time when you have been part of a very powerful conference where the Spirit of God was moving in a mighty way, and you were all excited as you could so strongly feel that your breakthrough was at hand? But after the conference, your life seemed to go in a totally opposite direction! Or have you ever received a prophetic word with your spirit bearing absolute witness that it is so, but then all hell broke loose afterwards. It is the intensity of the Holy Spirit that has led you into a wilderness on account of the unseen reality that you have experienced in the conference. Likewise, the prophetic word you received must be worked out in the seen world for the unseen reality of it to become a physical reality.

We learn in Genesis 1: 2 that the moving of the Spirit does not change anything; things only began to change when God spoke the Word. In the same way the Spirit can move mightily in a service, but it will not change anything unless we apply the word that was spoken. Thus a prophetic word will only be fulfilled when we speak and stand on that word. *And the earth was without form, and void; and darkness was upon the face of the deep. And the Spirit of God moved upon the face of the waters. And God said, Let there be light: and there was light.* (Genesis 1:2-3) Please note: Nothing changed when the Spirit of God moved upon the face of the waters; change occurred only when God said, 'let there be light'.

The wilderness is a testing season to purge our mindsets, attitudes, personality, character and the core of our beings to prepare us, *For we are his workmanship, created in Christ Jesus unto good works, which God hath before ordained that we should walk in them* - (Ephesians 2:10) All tradesmen are the workmanship of their mentors to prepare them to do the related employment of their trade. Please ask any tradesman how tough their training was, and then you will understand why they are good at what they do. Deuteronomy 8:2 clearly defines the purpose of the wilderness experience. *And thou shalt remember all the way which the LORD thy God led thee these forty years in the wilderness, to humble thee, and to prove thee, to know what was in thine heart, whether thou wouldest keep his commandments, or no.*

Jesus has made us kings and priests to our God and Father, to rule and reign the earth, which is our kingdom mandate; however, we need schooling for ruling and training for reigning. Take Prince Charles as an example: he was born to be a king, but he has had to undergo severe training and development to do the work of a king in his mother's kingdom. This is what Paul is saying in 1 Corinthians 4: 8 *You already have all you want! You have already become rich! You have become kings without us! I wish you really were kings so that we could be kings with you!* (International Standard Version)

Jesus made us kings. I also wish like Apostle Paul, that we were all really kings, so that we can rule and reign the earth. We are kings, but we all need to submit ourselves to the development process so we can apply our true kingship. Does it make sense that Paul says, 'I wish you really were kings'? We are already kings, but do we all have rulership over our thoughts, emotions, bad habits, the way we conduct our marriage and family life, our relationships, our finances, and also the kind of image we portray of the LORD and the Church at our workplaces, etc.?

THE "SPIRIT–SOUL–BODY" DIVINE ORDER POSITIONS US TO RULE IN LIFE.

Many of us operate in this incorrect order, i.e. body, soul, spirit; but we are designed to operate from our highest dimension, which is our spirit. And the very God of peace sanctify you wholly; and I pray God your whole spirit and soul and body be preserved blameless unto the coming of our Lord Jesus Christ. (1 Thessalonians 5:23) If we allow our spirit to thus lead our soul dimension, the members of our physical body will naturally become instruments of righteousness unto God. Let not sin therefore reign in your mortal body, that ye should obey it in the lusts thereof. Neither yield ye your members as instruments of unrighteousness unto sin: but yield yourselves unto God, as those that are alive from the dead, and your members as instruments of righteousness unto God. (Romans 6:12-13)

The wilderness processes us to function the way God has designed us to function. We are spirit-beings having a natural experience; therefore we function best when we operate in **this** order: spirit, soul, body. It is the gifts of grace and righteousness that position us for rulership in life. These two gifts manifest themselves from our spirit, through our soul, and then through our mortal bodies. However, if we are not rightly positioned - spirit, soul and body, we might miss out on the reality of what these gifts can do for us. The abundance of grace and the gift of righteousness to rule in life will automatically flow from our spirit-man into our soul-man, which will energize our physical body to take the necessary action to rule in whatsoever given situation or circumstance. For if by one man's offence death reigned by one; much more they which receive abundance of grace and of the gift of righteousness shall reign in life by one, Jesus Christ.) (Romans 5:17) But we have this treasure in earthen vessels, that the excellency of the power may be of God, and not of us. (2 Corinthians 4:7)

What we think creates emotion (which is energy-in-motion), activating our physical body to act in accordance to what we feel. Our physical body is the lowest part of our being, therefore it cannot please God; it profits nothing if it operates independently from our spirit-man. So then they that are in the flesh cannot please God. (Romans 8:8)

Our soul-man is at a slightly higher level, consisting of our mind, will and emotions, and our spirit-man is the highest spiritual level of our total being, which has the likeness and image of God. If we activate this level by being in tune with the Spirit of God it will automatically cause our mind to think wisely and positively, our emotions to be healthy and our physical body to act correctly. This is oneness in the true sense; therefore nothing will be impossible for a person who operates in this fashion. We may all be born equal with the same faculties, but very few of us exercise them to good purpose. The key to our success in ruling in life is to get all three levels (spirit-soul-body) to work in harmony. To do this they have to operate in the correct sequence – from the inside out. We will always enjoy perfect peace all the days of our lives, if we operate from our spirit-man. We tend to think straight when we are at peace with ourselves.

What does it mean to be at peace with ourselves? We are at peace with ourselves when our mind, will and emotions are in harmony. This is what we call soul-harmony. We are in turmoil or restless when we decide to do something that we did not thoroughly think through – this actually means your mind and will is not in agreement and it causes a lack of peace. This is the reason for second thoughts, which really means there was no first thoughts in the first place. Can you see the disorder when we are not rightly aligned with God's divine order of spirit – soul – body? Our wilderness is a kind of a workshop where the Spirit of God and the Word of God works in us in the midst of our trials and tribulation to bring us into this divine order.

Many of us however function on our two lower levels – body and soul or soul and body. Our energy in life is concentrated on the physical and the emotional, and we are concerned with physical needs such as having enough food, drink and sleep, and with having enough material possessions. We are also preoccupied with our emotional needs. And so our whole life becomes concerned with satisfying the central need to gratify our physical and emotional desires. The advertising industry understands this reality. All adverts are geared to the physical and emotional levels. The companies that are persuading us to buy their products appeal to our emotional level. We never see adverts geared to our mental or spiritual level.

Jesus is very aware of this tendency and instructs us saying; *Therefore take no thought, saying, What shall we eat? or, What shall we drink? or, Wherewithal shall we be clothed? (For after all these things do the Gentiles seek:) for your heavenly Father know that ye have need of all these things. But seek ye first the kingdom of God, and his righteousness; and all these things shall be added unto you.* (Matthew 6:31-33) It is only those of us who have been processed and sanctified in the wilderness dimension that will be properly re-aligned to function in the right sequence of spirit, soul and body. And it is only these who will really concern themselves about the kingdom of God.

THIS IS HOW WE OUGHT TO OPERATE IN THIS WORLD.

We are supposed to live from the inside out – this means we must start with the inner or spirit-man. This is why Jesus said – *when thou prayest, enter into thy closet* **(room)** *and when thou hast shut thy door, pray to thy Father which is in secret; and thy Father which seeth in secret shall reward thee openly.* (Matthew 6:6) It is during our private time with the Father that we receive revelation, insight, understanding, concepts, ideas and strategies. Remember the words of Jesus, **"I only do what my Father tells me to do".** We also need to seek counsel from many mature believers concerning the direction we sense from our private time with God. *Where no counsel is, the people fall: but in the multitude of counsellors there is safety.* (Proverbs 11:14) *Without counsel purposes are disappointed: but in the multitude of counsellors they are established.* (Proverbs 15:22)

Next is to call those things that we have received during our private time and that have been established by the counsel of many, as though they do exist. *and calls those things which be not as though they were (Romans 4:17b)* Then we need to take whatever we receive on our first level (spirit-man), to the second level by way of pondering, meditation and thinking on what the Father has revealed to us. It is on this level that we can begin to create a picture of what we have received in our spirit-man. In this way we can utilize our imagination to convert our ideas into visible pictures that will in turn activate our emotions. Genesis 11: 6 talks about the power of our imagination – it is saying to us, nothing will be impossible that we have imagined doing.

It is the intensity of our emotions that activates our physical level to take the necessary action to bring to pass what we have received in our private time with our Father. Emotions are energy-in-motion, which mobilizes our physical body to take action, since faith without corresponding action is dead. This is how we ought to use our three levels to work together in harmony. We are not designed to become successful any other way; instead our success should be a result of doing what the Father tells us to do. This eliminates strife, competition, jealousy and unnecessary envy that are so rampant in our society due to people who function primarily on their two lowest levels.

Chapter Thirteen

THE COMING TOGETHER OF TWO AGES

The Church in the past has lost Her influence over many things in the world by embracing a traditional mindset, a mindset which divides the world into two separate spheres of life, the sacred and the secular. The sacred, being the Church world, and the secular, being everybody else who lives independently from God.

This mindset has resulted in us, as the body of Christ (Church), losing our role in politics, economics, business, the music arena, sports, education, the medical arena, art and entertainment, etc, because we have separated ourselves from these 'wordly' activities. For instance, politics has always been viewed as a dirty game instead of being seen as dirty people playing politics. However, politics would change dramatically if god-people were in charge.

This traditional worldview does not exist in the written word of God, where both the Church and the world is the Lord's, and where we, as the body of Christ, have to do business in both. *The heavens are thine, the earth also is thine: as for the world and the fulness thereof, thou hast founded them.* (Psalm 89:11) This is the true expanse of the kingdom of God.

The Church is God's agent for the establishment of His kingdom in all the earth; therefore, the Church's influence in all the above mentioned arena is vitally important. God has already redeemed the Church; He now wants to redeem the world and the fullness thereof through us, and in these exciting end-time days, He is beginning to stir our spirits and to speak to us that our mindset be changed from our traditional mindset, or, for that kind of mindset not to be embraced at all.

In God's mind there are two kingdoms in the world – the kingdom of God and the kingdom of darkness. The kingdom of God is a single everlasting kingdom, whereas the kingdom of darkness is a kingdom of multiple fiefdoms that will eventually cause it to fall. *And if a kingdom be divided against itself, that kingdom cannot stand.* (Mark 3:24)

Apostle Paul tells the Colossians that it is God *Who hath delivered us from the power of darkness, and hath translated us into the kingdom of his dear Son,* (Colossians 1:13) and this transferring of many precious souls is happening 24/7 today, as the Lord is adding to the Church daily such as should be saved. The kingdom of darkness grows weaker as its citizenship decreases and the citizenship of the kingdom of God increases. All of this is leading towards the fulfillment of Revelation 11: *15b The kingdoms of this world are become the kingdoms of our Lord, and of his Christ* (The Church); *and He shall reign for ever and ever.*

I hope we see this, because we are trained in our thinking to expect the worst in the day and time we live, yet the biblical prophets would have loved to have been alive today to see the fulfillment of what they had prophesied under the inspiration of the Holy Spirit thousands of years ago.

There is no other kingdom that will ever rule over the kingdom of God – the kingdom of God is an everlasting kingdom, His dominion is from generation to generation with no other rule in-between. *And the kingdom and dominion, and the greatness of the kingdom under the whole heaven, shall be given to the people of the saints of the most High, whose kingdom is an everlasting kingdom, and all dominions shall serve and obey him.* (Daniel 7:27) *For the LORD most* high is terrible; he is a great King over all the earth. He shall subdue the people <u>under us, and the nations under our feet.</u> (Psalm 47:2-3)

We cannot claim that the kingdom of God is an everlasting kingdom if the saints of God leave the earth by means of a rapture. This would give the kingdom of darkness the upper hand to rule the world and the fullness thereof. Even common sense says this does not sound right. Everlasting means never-ending; never ever will the devil have full right and authority over the earth. The LORD has given the earth and the fullness thereof to His beloved children – you and me. The heaven, even the heavens, are the LORD'S: but the earth hath he given to the children of men. (Psalm 115:16)

Here is the paradigm shift that we should make in order for us to position ourselves for rulership. Instead of thinking in terms of sacred and secular, we should think in terms of the SPIRITUAL world and the NATURAL world. The spiritual world has been designed to rule over the natural world. Every born again child of God has the upper hand over the natural world and the natural people who have not yet been born again.

Through faith we understand that the worlds were framed by the word of God, so that things which are seen were not made of things which do appear. (Hebrews 11:3) The seen or natural world was not made by natural means; it came forth by what was spoken into the seen world. We are seated in heavenly places (unseen world) from where we rule over the seen (natural) world. Natural people are earth-bound – we on the other hand have complete access into heavenly things that we can bring forth into the natural world by faith.

Let's first look at the spiritual world and see how it has evolved. Both Adam and Eve were born into a kingdom age when they were formed by God. They received a kingdom which the Father had prepared for them from the foundation of the world. Then shall the King say unto them on his right hand,

Come, ye blessed of my Father, inherit the kingdom prepared for you from the foundation of the world (Matthew 25:34) Their failure to maintain or keep the kingdom has led to the loss of both it and their dominion. Through their disobedience they handed over to Satan their power to subdue the earth and to have dominion, losing their ability therefore to rule themselves from within, and creating a need to be ruled externally. This external rulership is only for a time. It is in place until mankind regains the power to rule from within, for the kingdom of God is within us.

The fall of Adam and Eve eventually gave birth to the age of law, which brought a curse into the world. *Nevertheless death reigned from Adam to Moses, even over them that had not sinned after the similitude of Adam's transgression, who is the figure of him that was to come.* (Romans 5:14) Moses was instrumental in bringing into the world the age of law, which is why it is called the law of Moses. The sin of Adam and Eve has brought a separation between God and man; God therefore initiated the law to be their schoolmaster during the age of law. *Wherefore the law was our schoolmaster to bring us unto Christ, that we might be justified by faith.* (Galatians 3:24)

The next age was the age of grace or Church age. *For Christ is the end of the law for righteousness to every one that believeth.* (Romans 10: 4) *For the law was given by Moses, but grace and truth came by Jesus Christ.* (John 1:17) The Age of grace is the current age we live in, and it is the message of the kingdom of God that will bring an end to this age. *And this gospel of the kingdom shall be preached in all the world for a witness unto all nations; and then shall the end come.* (Matthew 24:14) Then the Kingdom age will come, which will complete the life-cycle of the spiritual world.

A SUMMARY OF THE CYCLE OF SPIRITUAL AGES

KINGDOM AGE
LAW AGE
CHURCH / GRACE AGE
KINGDOM AGE.

THE PROGRESSIVE EVOLVING OF THE NATURAL WORLD.

The natural world evolved from the Hunter-Gatherer age, where humans lived in tribes, into the Agrarian age. All the people were equal even though you might have been the chief of your tribal group. Things changed in the Agrarian Age in the sense that there evolved a two-tiered society. The Agrarian age gave birth to two classes – the rich and the poor, or the haves and have-nots. Generally the king owned the land, and the peasants worked the king's land and paid the king tax by giving him a share of their harvests. In both these ages there was no money currency as people transacted with each other by exchanging what they had for what they needed. The middle class eventually arose during a transition from the Agrarian age to the Industrial age. These different classes do not exist in the Kingdom of God however, for we are all one in Christ, There is neither Jew nor Greek, there is neither bond nor free, there is neither male nor female : for ye are all one in Christ Jesus (Galatians 3:28) and Christ is all, and in all. Where there is neither Greek nor Jew, circumcision nor uncircumcision, Barbarian, Scythian, bond nor free: but Christ is all, and in all (Colossians 3:11) The truth of the matter is that these classes do exist in the world and worldly people are affected by this class system.

It is very interesting to note that the entire world and all the nations were affected by and witnessed the shift from the Agrarian Age to the Industrial Age. Jesus clearly said that the message of the kingdom of God will bring an end to the Church

Age and will usher in the Kingdom Age, which will be a witness to all the nations in our day. This shifting from the Church Age to the Kingdom Age will also include a dramatic shift from the Knowledge / Information Age to the Wisdom Age. Believe me, everyone will witness this paradigm change in the world. My heart jumps up and down every time I think, speak or write about this awesome change that will invade the world and all the nations in the world.

It was the Industrial age that brought light into the world and brought the world out of a dark age caused by ignorance. Where do witty-inventions and innovations come from? The world and everything in it belongs to God, even though man takes credit for the many inventions and innovations that have shaped and moulded our world. Every business idea and concept that betters the world and society comes from God, because He who started the world is faithful to complete it.

The Industrial age has changed the world dramatically. Thank God for Henry Ford who invented and designed the world's first car and the many other inventors that have been and still are used by God to enhance the world we live in. *That ye may be the children of your Father which is in heaven: for he maketh his sun to rise on the evil and on the good, and sendeth rain on the just and on the unjust.* (Matthew 5:45) Hear me saints, God does not work in the Church world only, He is mightily at work in the world He has created for our pleasure. We forget many times that God loves the whole of humanity; Christians do not have a monopoly on His wonderful love.

A kingdom mindset is a mind that thinks like God – God wants His children to be like Him. The heart of the Father is towards both the evil and the good, so we must not be quick to criticize people who are trying their best to make this world a better place, just because they are not Christians. It is really interesting to note Ecclesiastes 3:11 -He (God) *has planted eternity in the human heart,* (New Living Translation) - 'eternity' in the original language refers to the awesomeness we all feel towards creation and the sense that there is something more to life. Couple that with the mandate God has put upon mankind to 'look after the earth and subdue it' – is it any wonder even unsaved people are concerned for the health of the planet and all in it! Both unsaved and saved have this common mandate and awareness! Praise His Name.

It is a fact that good works cannot save a person – Jesus is the doorway to the Father. But neither should we use this truth to condemn non-Christians who have a tremendous heart of compassion and mercy, and who use their talents and resources towards helping those in financial and emotional need. They are managing to reach people in ways that are beyond the current scope of the greater part of the Church. Believe me, Christians who condemn these people, do not do the least of what they are doing. No works of the flesh can please God – yet work needs to be done to better the world. Who plays a key role when disaster strikes a nation? Humanitarian organizations do, and these are not necessarily Christian-based, yet they are being used by God, because God has a heart for hurting people.

Whom did God use to free South Africa from the apartheid system, which was the most devious and degrading system in the world? Mandela was well equipped for the task at hand and had a heart to do it. The eyes of the LORD are running to and fro across the whole earth to find a man or a woman to carry out specific assignments that would better the human race and the world we live in. If God cannot find a person in the Church who is well equipped for the task at hand, He will seek His world to find one. The Church in South Africa did not prepare and equip a person that was well able to set the South Africans free from apartheid, therefore God found Mandela. By the way, the Church has yet to produce a person with presidential qualities and competence to rule a nation.

THE INDUSTRIAL AGE IS VISITING THE DARK CONTINENTS IN THE WORLD.

I thank God for giving me insight and understanding as I observe what is happening in the world of business. I have been touched deeply as I have seen the heart of the Father. The world has again made a transition from the Industrial age into the Knowledge or Information Age, which means a change in the way business is done. This might take the world back to a two-tiered society (the rich and the poor), because the Industrial age that was responsible for the middle class, does not exist anymore as the world moves deeper into the Knowledge age.

People in general will be financially troubled unless they develop the necessary skills to create business in the Knowledge age, or grow other types of income apart from wages. Companies nowadays are very reluctant to invest their capital in a labour force as it is becoming obsolete with the introduction of computerised technology and robots. Companies in general are very happy with the utilization of machines and robots, because robots do not go on strikes, neither do they go on sick-leave or take holidays. This ensures profitability.

This is what I now observe: The world is moving on into another age called the Knowledge or Information age, even though some countries have not really tasted the Industrial age. Individuals in nations that have entered into the Knowledge age need to begin preparing themselves for it by making changes in their personal lives, as so many people are still unthinkingly dependent on their companies to provide them wages and other benefits.

A leaf needs to be taken out of the books of businesses and companies who over the last few years, have felt the pressure of constantly increasing demands for higher salaries and more benefits from staff, and have been thus challenged to think about taking their businesses into poorer nations where labour costs are cheaper. This makes perfect sense and has proven to be an excellent business move for many companies, but the real exciting thing is, it is the hand of God's mercy for the poorer nations, enabling them to taste the multiple benefits that the Industrial age has brought into the world.

Places like China, India, Malaysia, Ghana, Uganda, Kenya and other poor African nations are now attractive places to overseas businesses, because of cheap labour costs. Anything that can be manufactured in the West can be manufactured in China for less, and these products are much more affordable for the less privileged people in the world. So it is surely very insensitive, selfish and ignorant for the Church to focus on rapture teachings while God is busy upgrading these poorer countries by allowing big companies to invest in them so they might have an equal chance with the more developed nations.

The blessing of Abraham that has come on the Gentiles through Jesus Christ is meant for **all** nations. Why would we want to be raptured to go to heaven, whilst there are so many nations that are suffering under the destructive powers of poverty. Hear the heart of the LORD towards the poor through the prophet Isaiah. When the poor and needy seek water, and there is none, and their tongue faileth for thirst, I the LORD will hear them, I the God of Israel will not forsake them. I will open rivers in high places, and fountains in the midst of the valleys: I will make the wilderness a pool of water, and the dry land springs of water. I will plant in the wilderness the cedar, the shittah tree, and the myrtle, and the oil tree; I will set in the desert the fir tree, and the pine, and the box tree together: That they may see, and know, and consider, and understand together, that the hand of the LORD hath done this, and the Holy One of Israel hath created it. (Isaiah 41:17-20)

Is poverty more powerful than the power of God? If not, why do we want to give up on poorer nations by thinking that the rapture is the solution to all the problems in the world? The rulership of God, which is the kingdom of God, is our one and only solution. It was indeed very expensive in the earlier stages of the Industrial age to build infra-structures for factories in these poorer countries. However, globalization, technology and the world wide web made communication instantaneous anywhere in the world and has made the process of building infrastructure easier and less expensive, because it is now less time consuming. It also makes perfect business sense, because the price of cheaper labour outweighs the price of any infrastructure.

Have you ever noticed how quickly buildings are build with today's technology? The earth and the fullness thereof is the LORD's; therefore the LORD will make sure that all nations will receive equal treatment, even though it may be after many years of suffering. I hope I don't sound like Paul to whom Festus said with a loud voice, 'Paul, thou art beside thyself; much learning doth make thee mad. (Acts 26:24) I am not mad, I see the heart of God towards poorer nations. Jesus is not coming back for a weak Church that cannot bring order to a world filled with so much disorder, weird problems and much confusion.

And so we will begin to witness positive changes in poorer countries, changes that will enable them to be able to afford the technology and resources to make a transition into the Information Age. This will also be a sign that the Information Age is maturing in a world that is getting itself ready for the last transition into its final Age. This will be a transition from the Knowledge Age into the Wisdom Age.

A SUMMARY OF THE AGES AND LIFE-CYCLE OF THE NATURAL WORLD

> ➢ Hunter-Gatherer Age
> ➢ Agrarian Age
> ➢ Industrial Age
> ➢ Knowledge / Information Age
> ➢ Wisdom Age

The natural world has not yet completed its full life-cycle; therefore heaven retains Jesus, because the God we serve is a FINISHER. There has never been the slightest doubt in my mind that the God who started this great work in you *(and in the Body of Christ and in the world with no end)* would keep at it and bring it to a flourishing finish on the very day Christ Jesus appears. (Philippians 1:6) (Message Bible) NB! Italics is my own added words. Get ready, because we will now enter into the most exciting part of this book.

Chapter Fourteen

THE AGE OF WISDOM

The Creator of the Universe has established the world by His wisdom and He will also complete the life-cycle of this world by His wisdom. He hath made the earth by his power, he hath established the world by his wisdom, and hath stretched out the heavens by his discretion. (Jeremiah 10:12) This coming Wisdom Age will be a God-Age.

The wisdom of God is the rule of God; therefore we can conclude that these two ages are basically the same thing. The kingdom of God is the rule of God and God rules by His Supreme Wisdom. The world, who has denied God throughout all ages, will not be able to deny God in the Wisdom Age. The world and all its people will be unable to function independently from God in the Wisdom Age, which will be the Kingdom Age for the Church.

Throughout all Ages, people in the natural world have functioned independently from God by means of natural wisdom, insight and understanding pertaining to things like politics, economy, business, education, media, sports, music, art and entertainment and the medical arena. In fact, worldly people have generally taken the lead throughout the ages, in all spheres of life. Even Jesus said; For the children of this world are in their generation wiser than the children of light. (Luke 16:8b)

But the best wine has been kept till last – the natural world has indeed ruled over many things throughout the ages, but a sudden shift is about to surprise it. The last Age of the world is the Age where the Church will be in charge over all things, and all the nations in the world will recognize this shift. The following two verses show this shift of the nations' dependence on the secular, to a dependence on the Church, which is the house of God. *And I will punish Bel in Babylon* (the natural world), *and I will bring forth out of his mouth that which he hath swallowed up: and the nations shall not flow together any more unto him (World): yea, the wall of Babylon shall fall.* (Jeremiah 51:44)

According to this scripture, the natural world has been a source of leadership and strength to the nations, but the LORD has clearly said that the nations shall not flow together to the world anymore. Nations have always put their faith in the wisdom of men but the Bible clearly tells us *That your faith should not stand in the wisdom of men, but in the power of God.* (1 Corinthians 2:5)

The wisdom of men will fail the nations of the world; *And it shall come to pass in the last days, that the mountain of the LORD'S house shall be established in the top of the mountains, and shall be exalted above the hills; and all nations shall flow unto it* (the Church). (Isaiah 2:2) Thus an enormously important and highly significant shift will take place in the world during its transition from the Knowledge Age to the Wisdom Age. This shift will be a change in the flow of the nations and it will prepare the end-time harvest, when millions of precious souls will come to the LORD of the harvest, who is in absolute control of all events in the world, even though it might not seem so on the surface.

The so-called wise or prudent men of this world will call upon Church members and leaders to give solutions to life-threatening problems and challenges, just like in the days of Daniel. *And now the wise men, the astrologers, have been* brought in before me, that they should read this writing, and make known unto me the interpretation thereof: but they could not shew the interpretation of the thing (Daniel 5: 15) Then was Daniel brought in before the king. And the king spake and said unto Daniel, Art thou that Daniel, which art of the children of the captivity of Judah, whom the king my father brought out of Jewry? I have even heard of thee, that the spirit of the gods is in thee, and that <u>light and understanding and excellent wisdom</u> is found in thee (Daniel 5: 13-14). Then this <u>Daniel was preferred</u> above the presidents and princes, because an <u>excellent spirit</u> was in him; and the king thought to set him over the whole realm (Daniel 6: 3).

Let's have a look at what the LORD will do to accomplish the above mentioned:

For it is written, "I will destroy the wisdom of the wise, and I will set aside the understanding of the perceiving ones." Where is the wise? Where is the scribe? Where is the lawyer of this world? Has not God made foolish the wisdom of this world? (Corinthians 1:19-20)

- The LORD will destroy the wisdom of the wise.
- The LORD will set aside the understanding of the perceiving ones.
- The LORD will make foolish the wisdom of this world.
- People will ask where is the wise, the scribe and the lawyers of this natural world?
- The wisdom of this world will come to nothing. (1 Corinthians 2:6)

The wise men are ashamed, they are dismayed and taken: lo, they have rejected the word of the LORD; and what wisdom is in them? (Jeremiah 8:9) At that time Jesus answered and said, I thank thee, O Father, Lord of heaven and earth, because thou hast hid these things from the wise and prudent, and hast revealed them unto babes. (Matthew 11:25) This wisdom that was hidden is revealed to God's people, with God ordaining this wisdom long before the world existed, for our glory. (1 Corinthians 2:7) that we might reveal the glory of His kingdom. For His is the kingdom and the power and the glory, forever. Amen. To the intent that now unto the principalities and powers in heavenly places might be known by the church the manifold wisdom of God. (Ephesians 3:10) The manifold wisdom of God has been ordained before the foundation of the world to exalt the Church of God in the last days in the world. The world who has despised the Church over two thousand years will come to the Church with their problems and the challenges that they cannot resolve.

What will happen in the world when the wisdom of the wise and prudent will be destroyed and be brought to nothing? There will be terrible times of instability and turbulence in the world, because wisdom and knowledge is the stability of our times. And wisdom and knowledge shall be the stability of thy times. (Isaiah 33:6a) A lack of wisdom and knowledge is the very cause of darkness. This kind of darkness is very evident in Third World countries today where there is a lack of educational systems, revelation of the Word of God and deep poverty.

One night I stood in the streets of Uganda and I could literally feel and see the gross darkness in the nation. My heart broke and I thanked God for availing me the opportunity to share the Word of God there. I spread a level of light into that nation by the preaching of the Word of God that gives light. In fact it is the Industrial Age that has brought this very world out of a Dark Age in which there was an absence of wisdom to apply knowledge to better the world and the living life standards of humanity.

The lack of wisdom and knowledge in the world will produce terrible darkness. And they shall look unto the earth; and behold trouble and darkness, dimness of anguish; and they shall be driven to darkness. (Isaiah 8:22) But it shall not be so amongst the people of God, because there will be a great light on top of the mountain of the Lord's house. This will be because of the Wisdom of God that has been fore-ordained to show the powers and authorities in the spiritual world that God Almighty has many different kinds of wisdom. No wonder Isaiah saw the nations flow to the mountain of the Lord's house, as this is the only place where there will be light in the world. This will not be the first time that the world has experienced such a thing; it is written that there was a felt darkness in Egypt while there was light amongst the people of God. But now it moved between the Egyptians and the Israelites. The cloud gave light to the Israelites, but made it dark for the Egyptians, and during the night they could not come any closer. (Exodus 14:20) This very same thing will be recorded in history about the Church and the natural world we live in.

The foundation of the world will be shaken, because people have not built their lives upon the wisdom of God. Therefore we can conclude that anything that has not been built on God's wisdom has been built on sand, and according to Hebrews 12: 27b only the things that cannot be shaken will remain. Anything we have ever built that is not founded on kingdom principles or the wisdom of God, will be shaken and removed. Except the LORD build the house, they labour in vain that build it. (Psalm 127:1a)

We have all witnessed the radical changes in the world with the transition from the Industrial Age to the Knowledge/ Information Age. The latter has produced the most millionaires, multi-millionaires and billionaires in a very short period of time, and there is no doubt therefore, that the people in the natural world are expecting the next Age to be much greater than the Knowledge Age. Sorry to say, the wisdom of their wise men in which they have put their faith will be destroyed and brought to nothing. For, behold, the darkness shall cover the earth, and gross darkness the people: but the LORD shall arise upon thee, and his glory shall be seen upon thee. And the Gentiles shall come to thy light, and kings to the brightness of thy rising. (Isaiah 60:2-3) Then shall the righteous shine forth as the sun in the kingdom of their Father. Who hath ears to hear, let him hear. (Matthew 13:43) The best is yet to come...

WORLDY WISDOM VS. THE WISDOM OF GOD

The Apostle James defines worldly or natural wisdom as follows:

- ➢ Worldly wisdom is not from above.
- ➢ worldly wisdom is earthly.
- ➢ worldly wisdom is sensual and devilish.
- ➢ worldly wisdom produces envy and strife among earthly unregenerate men.
- ➢ The fruit of the wisdom of the world is confusion and every evil work. This wisdom descended not from above, but is earthly, sensual, devilish. For where envying and strife is, there is confusion and every evil work. (James 3:15-16)

The Apostle James defines the wisdom of God as follows:

It is wisdom from above
It is first pure
then peaceable
gentle
easy to be entreated (good for persuasion)
full of mercy and good fruits
without partiality
and without hypocrisy.

But the wisdom that is from above is first pure, then peaceable, gentle, and easy to be entreated, full of mercy and good fruits, without partiality, and without hypocrisy. And the fruit of righteousness is sown in peace of them that make peace. (James 3:17-18) These are the qualities that the wisdom of God produces in a person. They are also the qualities of a person who operates in the wisdom of God, and the qualities necessary to establish the kingdom of God to be effective in the coming Wisdom Age in the world.

Wisdom is the right application of knowledge or information, yet this definition is incomplete without the knowledge that Wisdom is a Person. The right application of knowledge produces fruit and incredible results. Worldly people do well in applying wisdom in all areas that pertain to life, but fail to apply knowledge to things pertaining to godliness. Most Christians on the other hand fail to apply knowledge to their natural life, since many of us could only relate to wisdom as a person.

This is very evident as we look at most workplaces or companies where the majority of Christians work under ungodly leaders. If we should do a survey in most business places, we would find that the majority of leaders and managers are non-Christians. I have personally been part of an interview panel to interview candidates for potential team leaders in the Company I worked for. It was indeed heartbreaking for me to observe that most Christians were unsuccessful or ill-prepared for leadership. We have a false balance of the application of knowledge or the use of wisdom, in both the Church world and the natural world. Proverbs 20: 23 notes that **a false balance is not good**. And we've got to have a balanced understanding of Wisdom if we want to experience lasting success in whatever endeavour or project we undertake in this world. We need to understand how to apply knowledge in all areas of life, and also learn to acknowledge and relate properly to the person called Wisdom.

The Christians will be the rulers in the coming Kingdom Age, which will also be known as the Wisdom Age. We will rule and reign, because we personally know the KING called Wisdom. By this time most Christians will have mastered the abilities that the secular people had in all the Ages of the world. For now we are in schooling for ruling and training for reigning in all spheres of life. We will be fully equipped and empowered to apply knowledge effectively in Business, Politics, Economy, Sports, Media, Education and Music, Art and Clean Entertainment.

The world will witness and enjoy a different kind of rulership than it has experienced during the rule of ungodly people. It is also true that some of the world's greatest thinkers (wise and prudent) will be converted to Christ as they become aware of their lack of Godly wisdom. Many of the world's amazingly wealthy people will also be swept into the Body of Christ during the great harvest, and just as the children of Israel crossed the Red Sea with the riches of Egypt, so a great transference of financial abundance will occur.

It will be impossible to operate successfully outside the person called Wisdom in the Wisdom Age. It will not matter how much you know if you don't know the Person called Wisdom in the Age of Wisdom. Act 6:10 gives us an account of Stephen operating in the wisdom of God - **They were not able to resist the wisdom and the spirit by which he spake.** This is what we can expect during the Wisdom Age – the world will not be able to resist the wisdom of God operating through us.

LET US ESTABLISH THE FACT THAT WISDOM IS A PERSON.

Counsel is mine, and sound wisdom: I am understanding; I have strength. (Proverbs 8:14) Glorious things are here spoken of this excellent Person – Wisdom, who is speaking here. It is Christ, in whom are hidden all the treasures of wisdom and knowledge. In whom are hid all the treasures of wisdom and knowledge. (Colossians 2:3) The Apostle Paul also states in

1Corinthians 1: 24b that Christ is the power of God, and the wisdom of God. The Wisdom of God is also known as the Word of God, the whole compass of divine revelation. It is Christ in the word and Christ in the heart, not only Christ revealed to us, but Christ revealed in us and through us.

Wisdom is the principle thing, Wisdom is the principal thing; therefore get wisdom: and with all thy getting get understanding (Proverbs 4:7) and the principle thing signifies the first thing or the foundational thing. Again, Wisdom is a person, as well as our ability to apply knowledge in all aspects of our lives. Christ, which is a mystery to the Gentiles is the foundation of a born again person's life, and without this rock solid foundation one cannot really stand the test of time.

The coming Wisdom Age in the world is going to be the greatest testing time that humanity has ever faced. The alarming question will be this: On what did we build our lives – on sand or upon the rock? Those of us who have built our lives on the sayings (wisdom) of Jesus Christ can be likened to a wise man, who built his house upon a rock. Those who built their lives on the wisdom of men, can be likened to a foolish man, who built his house upon sand. Wherefore if they shall say unto you, Behold, he is in the desert; go not forth: behold, he is in the secret chambers; believe it not (Matthew 24:26)

With the wisdom age will come great testing, which can be likened to rain descended, and floods and winds blowing and beating upon whatever all of us have ever built. And this word, Yet once more, signifieth the removing of those things that are shaken, as of things that are made, that those things which cannot be shaken may remain. Wherefore we receiving a kingdom which cannot be moved, let us have grace, whereby we may serve God acceptably with reverence and godly fear. (Hebrews 12:27-28) Those of us who have made wisdom our principle thing in building our lives on the sayings of Jesus Christ will remain after the great and awesome shakings in the last days of the world without end. Nevertheless the foundation of God standeth sure, having this seal, The Lord knoweth them that are his. (2 Timothy 2:19) As the whirlwind passeth, so is the wicked no more: but the righteous is an everlasting foundation. (Proverbs 10:25)

THE WISEST THING TO DO IS TO PREPARE OURSELVES FOR THE COMING WISDOM/ KINGDOM AGE.

Counsel is mine, and sound wisdom: I am understanding; I have strength. By me kings reign, and princes decree justice. (Proverbs 8:14-15) What does the last half of this verse mean to us who have been made kings and priests to God? We have to make godly wisdom the principle thing pertaining to all things in life, so that we might be found ready in the Wisdom Age to rule and reign in the world.

We need to carefully study the sayings of Jesus and build every part of our life on His rock- solid sayings. Therefore whosoever heareth these sayings of mine, and doeth them, I will liken him unto a wise man, which built his house upon a rock And the rain descended, and the floods came, and the winds blew, and beat upon that house; and it fell not: for it was founded upon a rock. And every one that heareth these sayings of mine, and doeth them not, shall be likened unto a foolish man, which built his house upon the sand (Matthew 7:24-26)

We need to search the heart of God, for every decision we have to make. The Word of God represents the heart and mind of God. Trust in the LORD with all thine heart; and lean not unto thine own understanding - (Proverbs 3:5) Any decision we make based on our own human understanding is equal to building on sand. Our lives should not fall apart even while the lives of people in the world are falling apart. On the contrary, they should witness our stability and want to seek counsel from us.

We also need to consider the Word of God, which is the wisdom of God, to be far more important than our daily bread. Rather go without food than without the word of God. But he answered and said, It is written, Man shall not live by bread alone, but by every word that proceedeth out of the mouth of God (Matthew 4:4)

And wisdom and knowledge shall be the stability of thy times, and strength of salvation: the fear of the LORD is his treasure. (Isaiah 33:6)

It is the wisdom of God and the knowledge of our Lord Jesus Christ that will bring stability in our times and in this crazy world and it will make us strong as we learn to treasure the fear of God. The fear of God is the respect we show Him through our godly conduct.

About the House of Alpha & Omega International

Our Corporate Directional Statements:

OUR PURPOSE STATEMENT:

To add real and lasting value to people's lives and to help, assist and support them to improve the quality of their lives on a consistent basis, so that they might become the people God intended them to be before the foundation of the world.

OUR VISION STATEMENT:

To be amongst the most relevant leading ministries in the world, which are socially sensitive and responsible in the development of people, communities, regions and nations to produce real spiritual growth and prosperity in all areas of life.

OUR MISSION STATEMENT:

To train, develop, equip and empower people from all walks of life, in all things that pertain to life and godliness, under the power of God, through the life-changing knowledge of our Lord Jesus Christ, the King of the Universe.

OUR CORE VALUES:

- Intimacy with God through prayer, praise and worship and the living Word of God.
- Our Apostolic Mandate.
- Our Kingdom Mandate.
- Family and covenant relationships.
- Character and personal development.
- Teamwork and team ministry.
- Development of all people and communities.
- Continuous improvement and excellence in ministry.

Winston Lucien Daniels
125 Verwoerd Street
Vanes Estate
Uitenhage (Port Elizabeth)
South Africa
6229
Tel: + 2741 9662283
Mobile: + 27 845662283
Email: kingdom@aomi.co.za
Website: www.aomi.co.za